MYSTICISM AND EXPERIENCE

Russell Hvolbek

University Press of America,® Inc.
Lanham • New York • Oxford

Copyright © 1998
University Press of America,® Inc.
4720 Boston Way
Lanham, Maryland 20706

12 Hid's Copse Rd.
Cummor Hill, Oxford OX2 9JJ

All rights reserved
Printed in the United States of America
British Library Cataloging in Publication Information Available

Library of Congress Cataloging-in-Publication Data

Hvolbek, Russell H.
Mysticism and experience / Russell Hvolbek
p. cm.
Includes bibliographical references and index.
1. Mysticism. 2. Experience (Religion) 3. Bohme, Jakob, 1575-1624. I. Title.
BL625.H86 1998 291.4'22—dc21 98-23954 CIP

ISBN 0-7618-1159-1 (cloth: alk. ppr.)
ISBN 0-7618-1160-5 (pbk: alk. ppr.)

∞™ The paper used in this publication meet the minimum requirements of American National Standard for information Sciences—Permanence of Paper for Printed Library Materials, ANSI Z39.48—1984

This book is dedicated to my wife, Naomi Seeger, my two sons, Julian and Maxwell, and my mother, Ruth Hvolbek. The book would never have gotten beyond my original composition without Naomi's love, her support, and the work she did editing and designing the final copy. Julian and Maxwell give me a ferocious appetite for existential experience as well as the desire to live up to myself. My mother has always encouraged my quest for experience and gave me the will to stick with the things that I started.

Contents

List of Figures	vii
Preface	ix
Chapter 1: Busy People Do Not Need Stars	1
Chapter 2: Experience and Knowing: The Mystical and the Conceptual	17
Chapter 3: Mystical Experiences	35
Chapter 4: Alchemy and the Inner Knowledge of Nature	47
Chapter 5: Spiritualism and the Inner Knowledge of Nature	63
Chapter 6: Madness and Knowledge	77
Chapter 7: God and Nature: Böhme's Mystically Derived Knowledge	87
Chapter 8: An Inner View of Things	103
Notes	111
Index	125

LIST OF FIGURES

1.1:	William Law's depiction of Böhme's Understanding	14
4.1:	The Alchemical Process	57
4.2:	The Scientific Process	58
7.1:	The Great Mystery of the World	89
7.2:	Böhme's view of the evolution of God	90
7.3:	The Philosophic Globe	94
8.1, 8.2:	Böhme's vision of the evolution of God from no-thing to some-thing	105, 106

Over the past fifteen years I have moved away from an idea of who I am to a feeling of who I am. I have been helped in this process by many wonderful people. David Luft and I have shared our nightmares and our dreams. Without his support, friendship, and perspective I would have remained more isolated and detached than I care to ponder. Amy Stewart, a spiritual light and a symbol of strength and caring, has given more to me than she thinks I have given to her. The experiences I shared and the quiet wisdom I absorbed with Hubert Holmes and Francis Foran at Pratt's Camp on the Little Southwest Marimichi in New Brunswick deepened my connection to the pulse of the uncalculated. Ann Manwaring and I shared many wonderful experiences together. Lastly, aside from the joy of teaching, my experiences in the classroom with elementary, high school, and college students have excited and inspired me.

PREFACE

As a book unfolds, it tells the author what he wants to say. Writing this book has helped me understand the experiences that tickled me with a knowledge that was not useful but life enriching. The most intense of these experiences occurred while salmon fishing in the New Brunswick wilderness, once while sitting in the Rocky Mountains of Colorado, and twice while sitting and talking with a friend on the seventh floor of a bank building off the 101 freeway in Los Angeles. My experiences might be called mystical, but to me they were intense existential events that cut through my time and my history to give me a new understanding of the world. I frequently wanted to justify and describe the knowledge that I gained from these experiences, but when I did so I found that a few people knew almost immediately what I was talking about but that most (the exceptions being many of the high school and college students whom I taught) had not a clue. This was probably because I did not know how to talk about the experiences convincingly.

Perhaps it was such experiences that drew me, while in graduate school at the University of Chicago, into studies of the losers of history (as one professor described them) as well as the winners: Johann Herder, Juan della Cruz, and Jacob Böhme, along with Galileo, René Descartes, Francis Bacon, Issac Newton, and company. I needed perspective, so I studied the scientific revolution and the battle against it by spiritualist and occult philosophers and traditional Aristotelian philosophers. The scientific revolution was essentially a knowledge revolution involving a new method for studying nature and a new theory of what constituted knowledge and how to get it. A small part of this revolution involved the great German mystic Jacob Böhme. His task was not against the development of the new world of science and its way of seeing and knowing. He recognized the beauty and power of science—what he called "outer" knowledge. Böhme wanted to enlarge the scope of the Scientific Revolution. His task was to explain clearly what "inner," personal, or mystical knowledge was and how it, too, was a necessary part of human life. My goals are similar.

This book is an attempt to talk about and put into perspective mystical (religious) and personal existential experiences and the knowledge such experiences give us. I also want to justify and champion the knowledge derived from those experiences. I do this first by examining the nature of experience as it takes place in science and the humanities and then by analyzing the mystical experiences of Böhme. Using Böhme to develop and explain the possibility of mystical experiences and then describing his experiences and the knowledge he acquired during them is a central part of this book. Not simply because it ties my experiences to an important figure, but because it gives me the opportunity to explain exactly what Böhme was talking about and why.

CHAPTER 1

BUSY PEOPLE DO NOT NEED STARS

> Somehow he had made me recapture an old feeling, something I had quite forgotten, the sheer joy of just moving around without attaching any intellectual purpose to it.
>
> Carlos Castaneda

This book discusses mystical experience and the knowledge an individual gains during such experiences. The fact that numerous people have had what are referred to as mystical experiences is well documented, but the nature of those experiences is not at all certain. Are such experiences chemical imbalances? Ghosts in the head? Subconscious projections? Or, and this is the most fundamental and important question that reports about mystical experience provoke: When a mystical experience occurs, does an individual actually receive an immediate, intuitive understanding of reality that is different from the rationally derived knowledge we learn over time? If this is the case, what is the knowledge one receives outside of time? If we do not approach mystical (or even religious) experience and the knowledge it purports to provide from this perspective, we will indeed be chasing ghosts.

In this study I assume that mystical experiences do occur, that they are not delusions, that they were once a common and more natural condition of humanity, and that as our rational conceptual powers have developed, many of us have become confused about the nature of mystical experience. I believe that mystical experiences are related to similar and more common (if less intense and profound) existential events that also cut through time, providing us with a vision of life different from our historically based, rationally developed comprehension of reality. Similar to the experience of stars or snowstorms that occasionally shatter the patterns of our normal thinking, a mystical experience is a somatosensory sense of things. Originating from a participatory relationship with nature and God, a mystical experience provokes an intuitive understanding of things. This understanding is different from the rational organization and subsequent understanding of things that occurs in the cerebral cortex.[1]

The book is an argument for pure experience and the immediate intuitive understanding of life that, as I will show, a mystical experience implies. It is not an argument against thought or reason; when dealing with the world, the daily stuff of our lives, we need to think. But in the part of us that needs to relate, feel, and understand the living of things, it is not the thinker who succeeds.

Tying the book together, although certainly not its only focus, is a discussion of the statements of the famous German mystic Jacob Böhme (1575-1624). While the nature of the mystical experience and the knowledge such experiences provide are the focus of the book, I use Böhme as a tether, keeping me tied to the events an individual claimed to have experienced and subsequently wrote about. By exploring the possibility that Böhme's experiences were truly mystical experiences and not delusions or contrived remembrances and by assaying whether his claims to know something as a result of those experiences have validity, I will say something about Böhme and the nature of mystical experience.

But before I explain Böhme's position in this book, let me elaborate on the perspective that must be taken if mystical experience and its claim to knowledge is to be understood at all.

There is a not so famous line in the movie *2001: A Space Odyssey*. A news reporter is interviewing one of the astronauts on a mission to Jupiter. The ship is equipped with the HAL 9000, the most advanced computer ever made. HAL runs the entire ship, plays chess, reads lips, and holds conversations. The reporter has just finished talking to HAL, who bragged about his ability to think and organize things and his confidence in the success of the mission. Finally it is the astronaut's turn. After a few perfunctory questions the reporter asks if HAL conscious. The astronaut's reply is instructive insofar as he suggests that HAL is as conscious as anything that is merely useful can be.

I bring this story up because I want to put mystical (call it religious or spiritual—all such experiences have a similar component) consciousness and experience into perspective. We have religious experiences only when the useful activities in which humans are normally engaged and the accompanying higher mental faculties (reasoning and concept formation) that allow us to reach our pragmatic goals are not dominant. Mystical experiences are infrequent because we are always engaging our rational powers in useful ways. Accordingly, mystical experiences provide a mode of knowing that transcends (or, more accurately stated, comes before) the rationally based, pragmatically driven paths to knowing that we are most familiar with. Let me explain.

Clearly, the normal consciousness of human beings is the thinking, willing, and rationality involved in the useful and pragmatic—the critical, logical, goal-oriented approach to things. In the useful activity of humans, thinking aims at domination and control of information. It plans, investigates, and wants results; it computes information for positive change, and it always has an objective goal.

Rational consciousness with its agenda of usefulness became a possibility for humans as the cerebral cortex evolved. The conceptual powers made possible by the growth of the cerebral cortex permitted humans to anticipate future possibilities, develop plans for better living, manipulate reality for their own benefit, and transfer their abstract conceptualizations from each to each (via language, art, etc.) and into reality. The pragmatic useful consciousness is about evolution. Humans transcended animal survival abilities and improved their living conditions by concentrating their mental powers on the useful. Since the development of the cerebral cortex, the normal condition of human activity (engagement in the useful) is attended to by all our rational powers. Our rational powers are directed toward and conditioned by our desire to understand and then gain control of our surroundings. All humans have a need and a desire to feel secure, prepared for the future, and hopeful about what will happen to them. Whether we are working hard in high school so that we will get into a good college or planning our career, financial, or vacation plans, we are using our rational powers pragmatically. Indeed, all the evolutionary conditions inherent in our lives demand that we be as pragmatic as possible; survival requires we concentrate our rational powers on such tasks.

I am not saying anything new here, but the point I want to stress is that the useful project and the consciousness that governs it and is governed by it (whether practiced by Neanderthals, rocket scientists, or businessmen) has always been the same. The rationality, focus, and orientation of individuals involved in projects aiming toward improving a position is identical: Critically analyze a situation, master the content of the situation, argue persuasively (arguing always takes place within the historical linguistic situation one finds oneself in, and all successful arguing is rationally consistent with the ethos of those one is engaged with), and seek to achieve a particular goal. The cavemen who sought to make their lives better by focusing on making better tools to kill, skin, and butcher animals were mentally engaged with reality in a way that is absolutely no different from a person developing a computer chip to place in a spacecraft or a student learning chemistry to get into college, to become a doctor, to buy a house, to raise a family, and so on. The level of rationality used by Neanderthals to hunt a mammoth is equal to that a rocket scientist uses to plot the path of a rocket toward Mars. The achievements of the modern world are not the result of superior rationality, but of the application of the cumulative knowledge of our predecessors coordinated by specific methodological principles and the scientific metaphysic.

The great technological, agricultural, and sociopolitical achievements of humanity are all a result of the fact that most people, most of the time, place most of their energy into useful, goal-oriented activity. The critical rationality that accompanies the pragmatic project has formed the basis of all the physical, medical, and technological advances humanity has achieved. When any person is engaged in the useful project of building a life, trying to get a job, or otherwise making life tangibly better, the orientation to reality and the rationality used to attain all such goals is the same. The recent developments in science, technology, and medicine are only evermore sophisticated, rationally based manipulations of reality. Indeed, the basic assumption underlying all scientific activity is that the world is somehow rational and lies open to rational analysis. But the advances in the scientific investigation of nature are not, from the standpoint of consciousness, any different from the useful orientation of the computer HAL. Such advances are not a surprise and certainly will never stop. This is what humans do best.

But this consciousness is limited and limiting. When people are involved in useful activities, they are oriented toward the world in a particular way, a way that determines consciousness along lines that permit further control and manipulation of reality. Things that do not contribute to the goal are ignored. This is the strength of the pragmatic consciousness. It advances itself. It is willing to change when business, environmental, or social conditions demand that change is necessary to further advance one's position. Nonetheless, the change is always for more control or to regain lost control. And it is a cumulative and self-determining activity; the more one engages in it the more one comes to engage with all things in this manner. A goal-oriented approach to life creates blinders. Whatever does not come within the parameters of the agenda is dismissed as irrelevant or recognized as getting in the way. We have all experienced the situation of wanting to go someplace and have something delay us. Our goal thwarted, we respond with anger and indignation at having to waste our time. When we say that we are wasting time, we usually mean that we are not doing what our practically and rationally constructed agendas have determined are important.

Until the seventeenth century, there were always factors such as inferior technology, confused investigative techniques, and especially, religious and social values that limited not simply the advance but the interest in pragmatic activities. The growth of capitalism and science has overcome such deflections from our pragmatic goals. The ideological values of capitalism encourage constant motion; capitalistic life is life in a continual quest for more. The values of capitalism instill in people a dissatisfaction with the present, and they encourage the utilization of all our rational powers on the pragmatic activity of acquiring gain. Within the ideology of capitalism, stars are unnecessary, unless they can mined for a profit.

Just as important for shaping our present consciousness is the creation of the epistemological and methodological principles of science. The developments of science since the seventeenth century have advanced our understanding and control of nature beyond the scope of what was ever imagined 300 years ago. Let's be clear here: The intellectual framework devised to study nature by early modern scientists (which businessmen and almost all academic disciplines have come to adopt) is perhaps the single greatest achievement in history. This is because it has allowed for a largely unimpeded development of the pragmatic project of control of nature for human betterment. In this sense, the development of science is an advancement of the earlier useful consciousness. Science has organized and focused all our rational powers on achieving a knowledge of how nature works; those rational powers, undeflected by other considerations, have given us great knowledge and even some control over nature.

However, reduced to its basics, the intellectual framework of science is really an editing out of all things that do not pertain to the specific goal of understanding nature through a set of methodological and epistemological principles. Combine these principles with a strict mathematical criterion of truth and you have the metaphysical soul of science; science is a set of beliefs that establish an orientation to the world. The growth of science is the growth of a particular set of metaphysical beliefs. The consequence of that framework is a rational distancing from the immediate, existential experiences one has with life. By controlling experience through a theoretical framework, socioculturally influenced experience is replaced by controlled scientific experience. Scientists do not need stars (at least when they are being scientists). Scientific experience is achieved by imposing an experimental and mathematical conceptual framework onto the useful consciousness and by seeking to eliminate from consciousness the personal, sociocultural issues that distract from the organized experience that is science.[2] Scientists do not need stars—they study stars. And they do so in a very determined way. The key to good science is to control the moment, to project an outcome, and to determine and then quantify the experience. When an undetermined event occurs in a scientific experiment, it may result in a new understanding of nature but the undetermined always occurs within a mostly determined situation.

The rational distancing from contingent reality that the intellectual framework of science permits and the success of the useful project of controlling reality that science has allowed has helped create a world that someone living in a cave would envy. But it has also encouraged a narrowing of life to the merely useful, a narrowing of human consciousness to the pragmatic. I suspect that when people condemn science for what they perceive to be a valueless world, they do not quite understand that science is merely continuing the useful consciousness in which humans have always engaged. Condemning science is like condemning human biology, human nature. To ask scientists to desist would be similar to asking our ancestors not to use fire or not to make better plows. It is the useful consciousness and the technological newness it helps advance that people are really questioning. Science is merely a refinement of that perspective. Science has helped elevate the useful consciousness to a higher plane. In itself, science is not the roadblock preventing comprehension of nonuseful orientations to reality such as the religious, the mystical, or the shamanistic; rather, the problem is in the success of science and the gradual usurpation of all consciousness into the useful project.[3]

There is an additional problem leading to the confused and shallow understanding we now have of things diverging from the pragmatic. The point of the religious, the mystical, or the alchemical is confused in the rationality of modern useful consciousness. From the Enlightenment to Sigmund Freud, the standard educated view is that the various religions propagated one false thing after another to a gullible public.[4] The position articulated by Freud is that religions arose as a result of fear, need, and want among primitive humans — pitiful people who were unable to accept the unvarnished truth about reality as we now know it to be, namely, as science defines it. Religion is a crutch. The religious explanation of things (and all mythical or occult explanations as well) is assumed to be simply a poor attempt by primitive people to explain things they found unexplainable. Freud painted science, or rather the mode of thinking that takes place in science, as the savior. Science has cleared up the confusion inculcated into the minds of primitive people by their religions. For the educated classes, religion is bad, shamanism and the occult stupid, and mysticism insanity.

There is some truth to the criticism of religion by so-called objective thinkers. Many of the activities of religion needed (and need) to be questioned, especially when they trespassed into the corporeal and social realm of things in an effort to be useful. The horrors perpetuated in the name of religion are well known, as was the Church's condemnation of Galileo. But the casual adoption of any simple historical assumptions as fact (false, inferior religion; true, superior science) is always misleading. More important, the problems created by the trespass have to be blamed on the interpretation of the religious experience, not on the religious experience itself. Surely there is a difference between religion and the religious, mysticism and the mystical, shamanism and a shaman's experience. Unfortunately, we seem stuck in our condemnations of the religious realm of knowing and being and are incapable of understanding religious experience at all. Anything associated with the religious is labeled as some earlier, lower level of thought. The religious is some kind of error.

The assumptions behind such assertions are insidious: Religious expression is the result of an overexcited, uncontrolled imagination; it has nothing to do with actual experience; present thought is superior to past thought; and all knowledge is cumulative, or it is not knowledge.

What has occurred over the past 200 years is the proverbial throwing the baby out with the bath water. True, the people who established and maintained religions often made a mess of the religious because they tried to incorporate it into the pragmatic project of humanity or vice versa, they infused the pragmatic into the religious. The religions of the world long desired and often succeeded in controlling the social and the intellectual areas of human activity. The inclusion of useful knowledge into the religious realm and the attempt to transfer religious knowledge into the useful sphere has always resulted in a diminution of the religious. And of course, religion needed to be questioned in the seventeenth century when it tried to determine the outcome of the pragmatic investigations of nature. But to say that the religious is bad and to deny the truths attained in the religious state because they do not adhere to the standards of truth established by the pragmatic project of science is simply to advance the hubris of one mode of knowing one over the other.

Let me make one more distinction: The religious is a personal existential experience, religion is the concretization and institutionalization of that experience. Religion is achieved through the creation and application of symbolism, metaphor, icon, architecture, image, and so on. Christ was the religious (had religious experiences); the Church institutionalized that experience. The *New Testament* literalized the experience of Christ. Cathedrals were the archtectualization of the experience of Christ. All were designed post-factum to say something about and capture the original experience so that it might be transferred to others. By concretizing Christ, human beings created Christianity. They "religionized" the religious in an attempt to permit others the possibly of having similar experiences. But all religionizing is merely an image of the religious. Religions are a social phenomena; the *religious* is a personal, existential experience, It is religions that get off base and confuse the religious issue because of various social, political, or other interests. The actual experience of the religious is and has always been the primary instigation of all religions. People can and do have religious experiences in connection with the activities withing their religions, but such experiences go beyond the hearing of a sermon or the reading of a sacred text. The religious and the mystical are noncumulative modes of knowledge.

Recognize the fact that we have confused religion with the religious, observe the success of the capitalism, science, and technology over the past 200 years and you can begin to see the difficulty the modern world has in understanding the religious. It is now difficult to understand what the actual experience of the religious entails. It is almost impossible to comprehend what the knowledge such an experience might be.[5] Similar to the experience of love, friendship, or any other quality experience—all impossible to quantify or control, and seemingly subjective—the experience of the religious does not fit within a rationally organized pragmatic orientation to things. The problem is not simply that we have reduced the value of anything that does not appear as objectively verifiable following the criterion of truth established by science to inferior status. The problem is that we have lost sight of what the religious experience is. Something has been forgotten. Something has been lost. This loss has had ramifications beyond the religious: It has made it difficult to account for the experiences of art, music, love, gardening, fishing, or the like in any other way than as forms of relative knowledge.

Despite the frequently chronicled litany of evils committed in the name of religion, in previous centuries it was generally religions that dwelt in and provided the forum for the nonmanipulative, nonpragmatic side of human experience and knowing. Whether people were religious or not, religions at least encouraged participation in a nonrational existential experience of things. This holds true today and helps explain the fact that a vast number of people in America seek out religion and occult activities.[6] The need is there. I suspect, however, that many of these religions offer more form than content; more the doctrine, less the religious. Form overrides content; the rational overrides the existential. This is unfortunate because the experience and knowing at the core of the religious (the mystical, the alchemical—even the artistic and poetic) has always been arational, nonconceptual, and not a means to some other end. The religious experience is not a useful one, it is an end in itself. It is openness to, not control of the other. It is the absence of self-striving and asserting, dominating and controlling.

Our denial of religion has led, really, to a loss of understanding of the religious experience. The issue is not simply that institutional religions are less valued in the modern westernized world, but that understanding of the experience and knowledge that is characterized as, but not limited to, the religious has been devalued and become an enigma. The "other condition," to borrow the Austrian writer Robert Musil's term, the condition of the illuminative, the meditative, the passive receptive waiting before the other, an inner knowledge and truth, has become an enigma to most people. The experience signaled by the body's reaction to an event has been neglected as the project to understand and then control nature, fueled by a mental orientation to things that is phenomenally successful in controlling them, has become ever more a possibility.

The very sophisticated rationality that has evolved to support and advance the pragmatic agendas of modern science, technology, politics, social issues, and business conceals the fact that the primal experience of the self with the other is always physical sensation, not rational interpretation: Feeling, not thought connects us with nature and each other. Conceptual representation and mental comprehension is always secondary. William Blake was right: religious truth is of the body, not the of intellect. The higher levels of mental activity processing an experience and then saying something rational or symbolic about it are not only different than the actual experience, they can begin to separate us from the experience. We have become a culture consumed by the concept, and the linguistic sign or representation of a thing has placed a screen between us and things. Thus, although language is a representation of experience, it is in feeling and experience that truth is found.[7] Pain and joy are truth. The advancement of the pragmatic consciousness coincides with the rationality that permitted it originally and is used whenever possible.

Thus, to return to the point of HAL, the problem with being merely useful is that in doing so one is involved in a particular mode of reasoning about reality, and this conditions a particular orientation to things. The rationality of the useful separates but gives control; feeling connects but risks losing control. Our rational powers also mask the fact that another side of being human involves the immediate existential relationships to life, the uncontrolled immediacy of experience that is always a mystery and sometimes points to a mystery beyond the experience. I am thinking about the nonbusy experience of stars, of mountains, of the eyes of a loved one, or of the religious. There is a knowing that occurs during such moments, although it has no practical purpose and it cannot be controlled for later use. It is a knowing of the self in the world, it is a connection. Such human experiences are not arrived at through the critical manipulation of nature or symbols, nor through goal-oriented activity. Only by stopping the useful project and its attendant mental activity that precipitated its development do mystical experiences evolve.

A mystical experience asserts itself against the belief that all knowing is noetic or the result of a rational assessment of things. William James made this point when he said that mysticism breaks down the dogmatism of rationalistic consciousness that would assert its own exclusive validity as the only legitimate form of consciousness. Mysticism argues against the mental idea of knowledge, against the conceptual as the only form of knowledge available to humans. In this regard, a mystical experience is a reconnection of the self to nature's pulse, a descent downward from a more complex mental orientation to things to a less historically influenced relationship with things. A mystical experience moves one away from an ideational relationship into a somatosensory relationship.

For reasons difficult to understand, I gravitated toward studying the strange, the useless, and the impractical (the mystical, the religious, the alchemical) in college and later in graduate school. Part of my desire was rationally based: Could the religious, something that was so much a part of the human experience, be so simply wrong as the modern rationally based, scientific experience of things suggested?

Could the entire inner life of humanity have been a mistake? I have always found it hard to believe in the intellectual superiority of the modern world. Whenever a thing is held so vehemently and with such assurance, something more than truth is involved. This rebellious streak grew, however, from my own childhood experiences with things. My experiences of the woods, fly-fishing, water, frogs, and snakes was not of pragmatic value. The results could not be sold, and they did not give me power or control. Rather, having been in conjunction with things, the experiences provided me with feelings, sensual relationships. Were they wrong? Were my senses and feelings a lie? Were the most palpable and life-transforming experiences wrong? I do not think so.

Do we need a purpose, a reason, a justification for these experiences? No. But if we want one, it is obvious—such human experiences offer a sense of relationship, of connection, and of the interrelationship between things. Busy people do not need stars; but if they are going to experience them, they will have to stop being busy for a moment. Unfortunately, the difficulties we now have are deeper than simply stopping the busyness. There is some way in which we have moved disastrously away from connecting and understanding the religious. We try to break the busyness and seek the woods, sunsets, connections, but we move away from the experience when we try to frame it or establish a meaning to it. Our seeking is itself an indication of how far we have moved from connection and how much we need it. Go into the woods with the practical intent to have an experience and you will have none, unless an event cuts through your plan not to be busy trying to have that connective experience.

The question remains for us: Are human beings who are striving to act on the world in terms of ends, be it as doctors, lawyers, scientists, politicians, builders, teachers getting students to pass a test, and so on, conscious? The answer remains: As conscious as something that is merely useful can be. Another question remains: Why have stars become unnecessary? And the answer remains: Because in the rationality of the useful they have no place (until they become useful).

Now let me put Böhme in context. Aside from the fact that he had a series of revelatory experiences and wrote about them, Böhme is historically interesting because he was by all other standards, a rather common working-class man. Born into a modestly well-off peasant family in 1575 in Görlitz on the eastern Border of German, he became a shoemaker, got married, and quickly became a father. His was not the spiritually wrought life of Juan de la Cruz or the young Luther. Nor was he theologically trained as Meister Eckhart was. He could read and write, but his education was modest.

Görlitz was a Lutheran city and Böhme was a Lutheran. Raised after the Formula of Concord in 1577, the dry religious practices of the orthodox Lutheran church did not suit him and, apparently, many others. The late sixteenth and early seventeenth centuries were filled with secret societies involved in occult and religious activities, and Böhme belonged to one run by the pastor Martin Möller. This study group, called the Conventicle of God's Real Servants, included many educated aristocrats interested in Paracelsian occult philosophy. Several became Böhme's close friends and supported him financially. And, while Görlitz in 1600 was not Wittenberg in 1521 or Königsberg in 1800, intellectual activity in the study groups was serious. Indeed, Böhme lived during one of the theoretically formative periods of Western history. Böhme's contemporaries included William Harvey, Johannes Kepler, Francis Bacon, and Galileo. If Böhme's statements are indicative of the general issues of the time, topics of discussion included not only the natural philosophy of Paracelsus, mysticism, and the radical spiritualism of Caspar Schwenckfeld, but the dialogues about modern mathematical science and cosmogony.

Böhme was seriously engaged in the intellectual activity of Görlitz and must have been a respected man. This despite the fact that his ability to express his ideas was far below average: His writings are some of the most confused, discombobulated, and chaotic collection of words ever put to page. When you try to read Böhme, you get a headache, you get angry; usually, you do not get very far. His ideas are abstruse, his language obscure; even G.W.F. Hegel, who spun a few heads himself, claimed that reading Böhme made him dizzy.

However, despite the convoluted expression and the terrible prose, the attraction of Böhme is that he had those mystical experiences and that he wrote down what he existentially experienced during those moments. Böhme had (or was given) an understanding of reality from a nonuseful perspective. Thus, a man who should have written nothing, wrote much. What he wrote about in remarkably creative ways was cosmogony, physics, and God. This bothered many people of his time. How could he know the things he did? His response was always the same: I did not learn it, he said, I was given it during a series of mystical experiences.

The experiences began around 1600, when he was twenty-five, and lasted until at least 1612. During that time he recorded his experiences and, with the help of several aristocratic friends—members of the spiritual study group—he had the writings put into a book, *Morgenröte im Anfang*, also called *Aurora*.⁸ The book was distributed throughout Görlitz and Böhme became an even more celebrated figure among the local intellectuals. The book also attracted the attention and anger of the minister, and because of its claim to superior firsthand knowledge from God, Böhme was banned from writing anything more. He adhered to the ban for several years, but then began to write and publish again. His return to writing resulted in his being asked to leave Görlitz by the local pastor.

Supported by his friends, Böhme continued to write and by the end of his life, nine years later in 1624, he had written more than twenty books and pamphlets. Locally famous at the time of his death, by the middle of the century his books were being widely translated and published by the Dutch and English. They inspired German Romantic philosophers (including Franz Xavier von Baader), English theologians (William Law and others), poets (Robert Browning and Theodore Roethke), and artists (William Blake). Figure 1.1 is William Law's depiction of Böhme's understanding. Hegel considered Böhme and Bacon the fathers of modern philosophy.⁹

There are three things that entice initial investigation of Böhme's writings: the claims behind the work, his juxtaposition of his theories and experience as different from yet complementary to those of the new sciences, and his physical and cosmological theories. Böhme claimed that his intuitive (mystical) experiences of nature provided him with a knowledge of the physics and cosmology of the universe. He was adamant that his knowledge was intuitive, a direct consequence of his experiences with God, and not a result of a rational reconfiguration of data or a construction on a previous set of theories. He was merely the spokesman of God, a "tool with whom God does what he wants." None of his knowledge was from "reason's work," but from God; he was "only a poor simple instrument."¹⁰

Despite his claim for a nonrational intuitive knowledge, Böhme was not an uninquiring man who just happened to be given a series of divine illuminations. He was concerned with trying to understand nature because, among other reasons to be discussed later, the cosmological theories of Copernicus had thrown his universe out of joint. These theories, which he accepted as true, disturbed him.

Consequently, Böhme spent a lot of time ruminating on how to reunderstand the universe in face of the new cosmology. Nevertheless, Böhme was not interested in rationally working out a new theory of the relationships between God, nature, and humankind spawned by Copernicus. Because of the historical traditions of alchemy and spiritualism that he had absorbed, his concern was with discovering an

14 *Mysticism and Experience*

Figure 1.1: William Law's depiction of Böhme's understanding.
Source: **The Works of Jacob Böhme.** London: M. Richardson, 1764.

inner, intuitive reunderstanding. It was his silent ruminations (perhaps the artisanal tasks of shoemaking were conducive to meditative states) that set the stage for his illuminations.

Thus, writing at the key turning point in the development of the modern world—when Galileo, Bacon, Kepler, Harvey, and Descartes were defining the theoretical principles and the ontological attitudes that set the stage for the development of a scientific knowledge of nature—Böhme was trying to understand how nature worked by sitting in fields, eating apples, hugging trees, needing stars, and having mystical, heart-changing revelations about the nature of reality. Unlike the interpretation of reality derived through the scientific method or those that resulted from the Church's ideology, Böhme was meditating on a universe he now recognized as disjointed. The attempt to understand a post-Copernican universe by eating apples, sitting in fields, and meditating conditioned Böhme's experience. Böhme argued that his orientation to knowledge was distinctly different from the one practiced by the rational sciences and that it resulted in a different knowledge.

The knowledge Böhme acquired was about the living relationships between things, the ontological state of things; his was an inner knowledge of what he called *Eternal Nature*. Böhme's knowledge of nature extends beyond the epistemological and methodological limits science sets to experience, beyond the realm of experience established in philosophy, history, and the humanities, and beyond the localized sociocultural values of his time. I place Böhme within the context of the early history of science not simply to put his experience in sharper focus, but to broaden historical perspective about the epistemological nature of modern science. Böhme was responding to the developments of modern science, not in a critical but in a supportive way. He juxtaposed his inner understanding alongside the rational developed knowledge of the new sciences.

Böhme also merits attention because what we can learn about him will help us understand other enigmatic historical figures. Böhme's descriptions of what he learned during his mystical experiences define an orientation that extends forward in time to Hegel, Blake, Martin Heidegger, D. H. Lawrence, and Ludwig Wittgenstein and backward to the German mystical traditions of Eckhart, the radical Lutheran spiritualists of the sixteenth century, and the occult and alchemical philosophers such as Paracelsus. His experiences extend laterally across the ages to the shamanistic, the magical, the occult, the alchemical, to the immediate existential experience primitive people had with reality. They also suggest what is at the heart of the experiences we seek when we walk in the woods, sit on the beach, go fly-fishing or skiing, or gaze at the stars. Busy, overly rational, pragmatic people do need stars—they have simply lost sight of this fact.

Chapter 2

Experience and Knowing: The Mystical and the Conceptual

> The supreme lesson of human consciousness is to learn how not to know. That is, how not to interfere. That is, how to live dynamically from the great Source, and not statically, like machines driven by ideals and principles from the head.
>
> D. H. Lawrence

To discuss the mystical, and we can include the religious, the magical, the alchemical here as well, it is necessary to say a few things about the nature of experience. Normally, we think of experience as moments in our lives: sitting on the beach, walking in the woods, going to a ball game, or eating dinner. But what we call normal experience is never simply the events we participate in; in addition to the external event, there is always an intellectual side to human experience: We filter the events that occur to us through the concepts or prejudices we have developed over the course of our lives.

In all human experience, there is always a bouncing back and forth between events and our conceptual orientations. The concepts we formulate to make order out of the vast complex of reality determine each of us in slightly different ways because all new events are judged by our mental orientations to things. Concepts are a stabilizing force because they regulate the influx of data and put it into a comprehensible form. The breakdown of our normal conceptual filters results in a feeling of displacement. If this breakdown is serious, it will force a withdrawal from normal life and the adoption of a new set of criteria to make living possible again. In the normal conditions of life, most of the events that occur to us are not, properly speaking, experiences at all; rather, predetermined by concepts or patterns of thought, most of the moments of life become a confirming of the intellectual screen we have developed.[1]

Our lives are more like stagnant episodes: long successions of activities governed by static systems of thought. We call this normal life. The mental screen of our prejudices dominates our day-to-day pursuits as we try to get on with the project of keeping our lives in order. This is why out-of-the-normal events, although sometimes horrifying, can galvanize us and make such moments much more memorable than the static patterns we normally live in. If the event is really shocking, our conceptual orientation may break down, quite possibly resulting in insanity. When a shocking event occurs, we are really experiencing more deeply because our everyday patterns of thought are disrupted. At such times, when what is experienced is not slotted easily into our ordinary concepts, we are forced to reevaluate our views. All experience that goes beyond the static normal patterns we have evolved results in tension. This tension is a result of stopping the normal patterns of our controlled episodic orientation to things; the concepts that gave order to our lives are no longer adequate to the primal experience at hand. Confusion results. But confusion, a breaking of the established conceptual patterns, is always the first step to a new knowing. An event that becomes a transformative experience is always a conceptual reorientation of the individual to the world.

In an experience that initiates reorientation of an individual to things, there is then a lack of control of life to the concept or to the patterns of thought that have governed our orientation to things. To have an experience requires forgetting the name of the thing being seen. In contrast to the normal project of humanity, which starts with the rational-conceptual, the theoretical, and seeks to control and manipulate nature, a transformative experience is a stopping of the mental. In such an experience, something new is received. The experience that allows for human growth and change is actually present only in a new connection to things, and a new connection occurs only with a stopping of the conceptually familiar.

Of course, our symbols and concepts are never simply our own but are part of the ethotic situation in which we find ourselves.[2] Through the symbols and concepts of our society or particular fields, we acquire a knowledge of and a particular relationship to the world. Such knowledge and conceptual relationships to reality become, as indicated above, a mode of experiencing reality. When one dwells long enough in a field—mathematics, chemistry, engineering, history, philosophy—one begins to experience reality in a particular way; the reality one experiences is guided by the historical-linguistic patterns of thought the individual has learned. Most of what goes on in schools does not involve transformative experience, but rather, the piling up of the information needed to create a particular type of experience or orientation to things. The learning of historical information, art history, scientific laws, or the ten things Plato said does not usually involve experience, but is better understood as the building up of the sociointellectual filters necessary for seeing reality according to the topical view of things. The view of things in special fields, in science, history, mathematics, and other areas of higher education, becomes a reality for the practitioners who, because of their unique mental filters, exclude everything else. Most of the daily accomplishments of science, history, or psychology are not the result of experience, but of the accretion of another bit of knowledge. A transformative experience in science, as in life, is never science itself (according to the acceptable patterns of thought), but a new condition of science. The real leaps in all types of understanding are like poetic truths that break the script that previous rational activity had been adding on to.

Furthermore, when one has a new experience, one is receiving, not determining something. With a new experience, something comes to us and shatters our previous conceptually conditioned understanding, waking us to a new understanding. During an experience, the other gives us something because we have our conceptual filtering systems shut off or thrown into question. All creativity involves an absence of thought and an allowing of the world to reveal something new. Art is not made up, it is drawn forth from an event. Were the mental filters firmly in place and working properly, the event would become part of the normal patterns of our thought. The more rigidly doctrinal one is, the fewer one's new experiences. Thus, every new experience is not simply a new understanding, but also a change of heart.

Aside from the understandings acquired by individuals during the course of their lives, the major modes of gaining and transmitting the collective truths and knowledge of human experience to individuals are the sciences, arts, and humanities. Truths derived from the experience of reality as determined by science are different from those received through the humanities and the arts. Science seeks an objective knowledge of the workings of nature; the humanities seek an understanding of the human interpretation of the experience of things.

The difference between the truths of science and those in culture, the arts, and the humanities is not simply their mode of description, and it is certainly not that one has more and the other less rationality. The difference lies in their mode of experience as determined by their conceptual presuppositions. An underlying and usually unarticulated metaphysic rules both types of consciousness. Both are involved in a selective interpretation of reality (they investigate only certain aspects of reality), but the mode of experiencing things is differently established in the sciences than it is in the arts and humanities.

The limits set to the experience of nature, which have resulted in the current vast body of scientific knowledge, were first established in the scientific revolution of the seventeenth century. At that time, the methodological practices and epistemological assumptions necessary to acquire an understanding of how nature works were established by the fathers of modern science. Since then, science has replaced the Church as the arbiter of what is fact and what is fiction. This was not simply a development of the logical and rational capacities of humankind. It was a redefining of what was the best way to experience nature so as to get a knowledge of how it worked. Rational activity was never higher than in the Middle Ages, but it was limited to the conceptual patterns and the religious and social agendas determined by Church history; Church history, with all its attendant desires, goals, traditions, and prejudices, determined the objects of study and the way in which human reason would be directed.

Since the seventeenth century, the discourse of the modern world has been conditioned by the epistemological values of science. The scientific revolution established a new way of thinking about reality and a new criterion of truth. Both the mode of thinking and the criterion of truth now extend beyond the parameters of science and pervade and influence all Western modes of thinking. The scientific epistemology created a mode of experience, and this mode of experience has extended far beyond its original borders; science has become the discourse of the modern world.[3] Scientific thinking is the intellectual framework that underwrote and continues to underwrite the project of the modern world. Understanding how nature works, controlling the environment, developing new and ever-improved machines, advancing our knowledge of physics, biology, and medicine, and the like to make human life easier and better has become a project of humanity. In the quest to understand how nature works, science is a refinement and continuation, albeit the most successful, of the practice of measuring, calculating, and trying to understand and control reality that humanity began to engage in as soon as the cerebral cortex advanced enough to permit an escape from immediate nature.

The achievements of science are the result of an epistemological and methodological belief system that frames the parameters of human experience. This framing, which creates a particular orientation to the study of nature, includes (1) a rejection of immediate empirical experience as a source of knowledge, (2) the adoption of a unique theoretical (mathematical) stand before things, and (3) the belief that adoption of these basic theoretical and methodological principles results in an objective, neutral, value-free form of knowledge.

The mode of experience we call scientific could not have begun until the two epistemological presuppositions that had governed the Western experience of nature for centuries were removed. It was Galileo who recognized both problems and in one great letter and one great book,[4] pointed out that it was unnecessary to fit the study of nature into the basic premises of the Bible and that a strictly empirical (Aristotelian) approach to the study of nature was an inappropriate and inefficient way to acquire knowledge of nature.

The rejection of the assumption that knowledge of nature had to coincide with the premises of the Bible and the Church marked the absolute juncture between the medieval and modern worlds. This is because the basis for determining what society would hold as true shifted away from the social organization (and organizer) that had been the final arbiter of thought (with all its attendant beliefs) for centuries to a new intellectual organization of what was important. Intellectual activity was now free not only from religious premises, but more important, from the connections with traditional modes of experiencing reality through involvement in and dialogue with tradition. A significant aspect of the scientific revolution was a shattering of the dialogical, hermeneutic approach to the experience of nature. Discourse about nature, as about religious practices, had been for centuries a conversation based on the writings of old masters: Aristotle, Galen, Ptolemy, and others. Galileo and others questioned Aristotle and the dialogue based on his works that had governed understanding for several hundred years.

The second difficulty with pre-Galilean approaches to the study of nature had to do less with guiding principles and much more to do with their lack; the problem was too great an involvement within the world, too much of an unquestioned empirical approach to the study of nature. The theoretical distancing necessary to acquire an objective knowledge of nature had not yet been fully understood or articulated. The point here is that a purely empirical approach to the study of nature is always anthropocentrically guided and leads to basic errors such as believing that the sun goes around the earth. Moreover, the flux and flow of everyday sense experience is vastly confusing. Prescientific descriptions of reality did not adequately filter sense experience through a set of organizing principles; they let too much life, too much nature come into their vision and their descriptions. Witness the writings of even such a mind as Johannes Kepler, whose three cosmological laws are buried within thousands of pages of additional, largely superfluous information. It was for this reason that Kepler, despite his achievements, was a medieval man and Galileo a modern man.[5]

The advancement of science was made possible by the recognition that (1) new, nonreligious filters had to be created to put the vast chaos of life experienced within the world into sharper focus; observation had to be guided by a different set of principles; (2) the significant object of investigation was the subtext beneath the flux and flow of everyday experience, not immediate experience; and (3) the language used to discuss, describe, and ultimately, to think about reality had to be more exact, less dialogical; it was necessary that mathematics become recognized as the language of nature, that is, science. Perhaps the most significant achievement of seventeenth century science was the creation of a new epistemology and methodology to guide experience, a change from words to signs, and the application of mathematical notations to describe and analyze reality. As Galileo noted, although humans are incapable of ever attaining the extensive knowledge of God, they can certainly know some things as well as God does. For example, two plus two is four.

The effect of these changes was not simply a theoretical reorientation but the creation of a new consciousness. By altering the intellectual screens used to experience reality and by creating and adopting a new language with which to think about things, early modern scientists established a new noetic field of living between themselves and things. The development of modern science was an ontological and an existential event, not merely a theoretical one.

Another achievement of early modern science was recognizing that within the natural language of everyday speech were prejudices that influenced understanding and an inexact use of language that prevented unambiguous knowing. Everyday speech, as Bacon recognized in 1620, was fluid, inexact, ambiguous, and influenced by idols that guided thinking along particular paths.[6] Half a century later, the members of the Royal Society (the English scientific organization created to guide the advancement of science) struggled with creating a more exact and scientific nomenclature and called for a more clear and precise use of speech. The essence of this call was a change from words to signs, symbols, formulae, and mathematical notation. Isaac Newton's efforts to define the scientific conception of time and space is illustrative. He recognized that time, space, place, and motion were not very well known, and that

> common people conceive those quantities under no other notions but from the relation they bear to sensible objects. And thence arise certain prejudices, for the removing of which it will be convenient to distinguish them into absolute and relative, true and apparent, mathematical and common.[7]

Newton moved from the ambiguous meanings of space and time as used in everyday speech to an unambiguous scientific meaning. Newton's effort to change word to sign is at the basis of all concept formation in modern science. A sign means one thing and that alone; a word is fluid. The problem here, as Gadamer developed, is that whenever words assume a mere sign function, the "original connection between speaking and thinking. . .has been changed into an instrumental relationship."[8] Scientific language does not seek to embrace everything, but to selectively approach the causal relationships between things. The scientific world is a different linguistically schematized experience of the world than the world of everyday speech.

More than anything else, the inclusion of mathematics as the language of science determined the orientation of scientists. All the fathers of modern science except Bacon were mathematicians and the filter for judging what to study was mathematics. God, too, became a mathematician who wrote the language of nature in mathematical terms. The language of science also had to be mathematics because mathematics was objectively true. Making mathematics the language of science allowed scientists to eliminate the problems of spirit, human feeling, and the like that marred previous efforts to say something concrete about how nature worked. This meant, as Descartes made clear, that one filtered out all objects of study except "material things" and retained only those aspects of things that could be "considered as the objects of pure mathematics."[9] You had to conceive of a neutral world of pure matter shorn from everyday experience that could be mathematically organized and quantified.

Knowledge of nature had to come before investigation of nature; theory had to precede and guide experience. Intentionally and by virtue of its own success, as the discourse of the modern world evolved, what occurred was a "passage from what one might call a discursive exchange within the world to the expression of knowledge as a reasoning practice upon the world."[10] More than anything else, the development of science is characterized by the establishment of mathematically based theory to guide the study of sense experience. Science reduces the status of raw sense experience to the dubious and the misleading.[11]

Galileo defined this theoretical position in his *Dialogue Concerning the Two Chief World Systems*. In the key passage of the book, Salviati (alias Galileo) is trying to teach the simple minded Aristotelian and sense-based realist how to see correctly, that is, scientifically. He has asked the empirically minded Simplicio to imagine an idealized situation and figure out what would happen.

> Suppose you have a plane surface as smooth as a mirror and made of some hard material like steel. This is not parallel to the horizon, but somewhat inclined, and upon it you have placed a ball which is perfectly spherical and of some hard and heavy material like bronze. What do you believe this will do when released . . . Remember that I said a perfectly round ball and a highly polished surface, in order to remove all external and accidental impediments. Similarly I want you to take away any impediment of the air caused by its resistance to separation, and all other accidental obstacles, if there are any.[12]

Simplicio replies, having got the image, like any high school student would, that the ball will roll down the incline, accelerating continually. If it were a perfectly level plane, the ball would stay still unless pushed; if pushed, it would maintain the speed given by the force forever.

The point of Galileo's thought experiment is that if you really want to understand how nature works, you have to get rid of the external things that disrupt your vision of reality and imagine the idealized reality behind the chaos of the everyday.

The next step was to prove the conception through specifically designed experiments that measured a predetermined set of events. Scientific experiments are idealized microsituations, controlled experiences. Behind all scientific experiments is a theory or hypothesis. An artificial situation is then designed to mirror nature without the complex variables found in normal reality, and as with all useful activity, a particular result is expected. An experiment is always created to prove that which has been previously imagined and assumed. Therefore, an experiment cannot be set up unless one has already assumed a particular truth about reality. It is the fortuitous occasion when something different from the expected result occurs; this might occasion a new experience—if the individual is open to it—and result in a new understanding of nature. The discovery that light is a wave and a particle occurred when scientists were trying to prove light was a particle.

This ideational aspect of basic science was even held by Galileo's opposite, Bacon, the supposed empirical inductive side of the scientific revolution. Bacon, too, recognized that undiluted sense experience was not the way to acquire a knowledge of how nature worked. A strict empirical approach to nature, wherein one adds one observation to another and then another, leads simply to large amounts of observations. A synthesizing perspective is necessary to select and order the observations in terms of importance and toward an end. "To the immediate and proper perception of the sense," Bacon said, "I do not give much weight; but I contrive that the office of the sense shall be only to judge of the experiment, and that the experiment itself shall judge of the thing."[13] Thus, the senses judge the results of the experiment through some form of measurement; the experiment, an attempt to prove a theory, assumes a preformed truth about nature.

In a scientific orientation to reality, as Werner Heisenberg put it, "immediate experience is replaced by idealized experience which claims to be recognized as the correct idealization by virtue of the fact that it allows mathematical structures to become visible in the phenomena."[14] Heisenberg went on to explain that what determines the scientific perspective is a "demand for precise experimental conditions, accurate measurements, an exact, unambiguous terminology and a mathematical presentation of the idealized phenomena."[15]

Early modern science made one other significant claim for its epistemology that helped determine the experience of things: If adopted, it would allow people to gain a knowledge that was free of values; scientific modes of knowing were objective, not subjective or socioculturally determined encounters with reality. Unlike the Church, for example, which had a social agenda and a set of presuppositions that influenced its knowledge claims, the fathers of modern science maintained that their epistemology gave a neutral knowledge of reality because it eliminated human issues and social concerns from its investigations. Within the ideology of science, truth was separated from value; scientific knowledge was objective knowledge precisely because it was value-free. It was not trying to advance any social or religious agenda, and it did not consider human, personal, or social issues in its quest for truth. Hence, the scientist's inherent suspicion of anthropomorphic knowledge claims.

However, the claim that scientific knowledge was value-free was itself value-full. There are no value-free observations! What Galileo and Descartes were saying was not that science was value-free but that it was not concerned with social, religious, and personal human values because it had set up a new set of values. Science was above the social, above the personal. Scientific truth stands independent of social opinion. When you adopt the scientific epistemology, you check your personal and social values at the door of the lab and accept a new set of values. These claims of early modern scientists are maintained by contemporary scientists.

The Values of Science

We now know that these claims are misleading on at least two levels: Historical investigation has shown that all scientific investigations and descriptions of nature are culturally influenced. Our culture predisposes all people, including scientists, to see the world in a certain way. Furthermore, although unconcerned with social, religious, and personal values, science has very strict values within the parameters of its own investigations. That is the key. Science set up parameters for itself and within those parameters its values are obvious: lie, fake your data, get caught at it, and you will quickly experience the moral wrath of your fellow scientists. Scientific values are very clear and distinct and are taught to school children every day.

Moreover, there is a value to the value of having a supposedly value-free orientation to experience; namely, that it allows an unsympathetic approach to reality. This is a valuable aspect of modern scientific modes of experience. It is not neutral. Like all values, a "value-free" value creates an attitude, an orientation, and certain expectations; it creates a realm of experience. A person, an animal, and even an object is seen differently when it is approached with sympathy rather than with indifference. One connects with that which one approaches sympathetically; one critically analyzes only that which one approaches a neutral manner. "Neutral" knowledge is not really neutral; it is, rather, knowledge that sits securely within a particularly ideological context (i.e., concerned with outer, as Böhme put it, rather than an inner truth).

Science is simply the best set of conceptual parameters ever established for guiding experience so that what is experienced leads to an understanding of the causal relationships of things occurring in space and time. The scientific mode of experience has advanced the human project of understanding and controlling nature better than any other. But, and this is the point I want to make, as the conceptual values of science are adopted by individuals and used to organize our experience of reality, they become more than just a system of thought. They become a mode of consciousness. A way to see and then to think about things is a way to be with things. Science is not simply a method used to learn about nature, it is an ontic condition. Learn to see scientifically and you have learned an orientation to the world. The scientific consciousness is gradually becoming the consciousness of the modern world, and the great successes of science and the attendant developments of technology, farming, medicine, and so on can be attributed to dwelling within this consciousness.

Let me make one more point. Creativity exists throughout the fields of science but it exists within the parameters of scientific experience. All really creative understandings within science, as with any creative experience, originate in the gut. The gut is the source of a breakdown of former scientific truths and a leap to a new truth; such are experiences to any scientist. But that experience, too, is within the sphere of understanding determined by the premises of science. Even Einstein, whose frequent leaps of thought were the result of an experience that transcended the mere accretion of knowledge common to most scientists, could not have had those leaps without first being deeply absorbed in the thought of previous physics. When scientists have an experience, that experience takes place within the mental parameters set up to determine scientific experience: Any experience in science is part of science itself, but it is also a new condition of it.

Experience in the Humanities

Compare this to the mode of experience leading to truth in the humanities or the arts. Like the sciences, the humanities set limits to the modes of experience. These limits are established by the historical traditions of the humanities themselves, that is, they involve the historical traditions of humanity. Naturally, one also brings to the humanities the personal understandings and biases one has acquired over time. The experience of the humanities differs from those in the sciences, not in terms of the dialectical process of understanding, but in the mode of relationship one must establish and the goals one seeks. In the humanities, the personal prejudices and concepts of the individual as determined by the sociocultural milieu are juxtaposed with the object of study, not as opposites distant from the tradition but as part of a process. When you attempt to understand in the humanities, you place yourself within the process of tradition, you dwell within the linguistic or artistic historical traditions (the text, the art, the poetry). And you do this with your own historically developed and determining biases.[16] In this process of understanding, the connecting link between self and object is the natural language one is familiar with. In the experience of the humanities or the arts, the natural language is the medium that connects the self-concepts that have guided interpretation and the conceptual expressions of the individual to what one is reading, listening to, looking at.

Studying the humanities is important not because people have to learn about George Washington, Simone de Beauvoir, Luther, or anyone else. Such "have to's" are usually social issues. More important, when you are reading, you are engaged in a pattern of thought, you are involved in a mode of thinking and seeing.[17] This mode of thinking is itself a historically conditioned, linguistically derived presentation of a subject. "The mode of being of tradition [the humanities] is . . . not sensible immediacy. It is language, in interpreting its texts the hearer who understands it relates its truth to his own linguistic orientation to the world."[18] Thus, when you get something from a philosophical truth, you receive something that changes your sociolinguistic understanding, your understanding of humanity. The goal of experience within the humanities is human growth and change. The goal is not, as it is sometimes presented, control of the truths of a philosopher so that one can argue well, nor is it control of nature. Certainly, people have used philosophy and literature as a tool of social oppression or exclusion, and most of what passes for the humanities in schools has to do with educating an individual into a particular social ideal. Granted, also, that educators usually think of history, literature, and the arts as a constructive process: We form better citizens by teaching them one particular ideology or another. But, at its core, studies in the humanities are destructive, not constructive. When you understand something about philosophy, art, or literature, you have had a personal experience, you have your prejudices broken (deconstructed) and then expanded (constructed).

The objective is not to teach a conservative or liberal or whatever value, it is to question the values one has adopted over time. In this sense the process of understanding in both humanities and science is always destructive of previous concepts, then constructive. The destructive part is the experiential part. However, new understanding in the humanities is a broadening of one's personal prejudices, not simply an increase in the objective knowledge of the past. In the dialectic of experience in the humanities, the one who has experienced has turned in upon himself or herself and become aware of his or her own experience.[19] In the humanities, the practical side to experience is human growth and change in terms of the breaking down of old prejudices and the creation of new ones. In the dialectic of experience in the humanities, the individual's personal comprehension of the experience of being human is changed, because, in the dialogue of the self with the painting, text, or poem, any experience is a reevaluation of personal meaning as derived from one's own traditions, one's past sociohistorical understanding.

Contrast this to the dialectic of experience in the sciences. Here the one who experiences turns on a knowledge outside the self and changes that knowledge. A new understanding of the workings of a DNA molecule results in a change in the scientist's "scientific" experience of nature. His or her scientifically affected consciousness is altered. The scientist is affected. It is certainly true that scientific training results in a specific orientation to the world, and therefore, a new scientific understanding will result in a change in the scientist. But the change is within the parameters of science. What is won through the advancement of the scientific mode of experience is a knowledge about the physical workings of nature. What is won in the humanities is a connection to the conceptual expressions of other humans, a connection to tradition, to civilization in the broadest sense of that word. What is lost in both is a connection to the nonscripted nature of the human being to nature, to the sensible immediacy of experience.

Perhaps the distinctions I am making between scientific experience and experience within the humanities could be better explained by comparing the teaching of science with the teaching of the history of science. Courses in science are designed to impart to students the modern scientific conceptions of nature, how nature works, and how humans can control nature. Science courses in the modern educational curriculum are much like courses the Church taught on Christianity in the Middle Ages: they are not critical, they are designed to bring students into the ethos of the scientific (and therefore the modern) world. Courses on science teach the modern, scientific way of perceiving reality; they intend to foster and advance the scientific perspective. They are designed to increase the knowledge we have about nature. Generally, you do not question the facts of science.

A course on the history of science, however, has a completely different objective. It is not designed to present students with the truth about how nature works, nor does it attempt to inculcate students into the scientific community. Rather, the starting point for courses on the history of science must be to make people aware of the sociohistorical forces that have helped form their perceptions, and it must offer them an intellectual basis for critically analyzing the perceptions they assume to be true. Then they might respond to the world rather than be a particular response of the modern world. Unlike science courses that offer an answer to how nature works, the project of a history of science course is to approach the scientific perspective, science itself, as a question (and an ongoing question at that), not an answer. Thus, when one acquires a new truth in science, one is furthering the scientific perspective; when one acquires a new truth in the humanities, one is changing a sociocultural perspective.

The attempt to make the humanities into the human sciences by applying the criteria of experience of science to history, anthropology, literature, and so on changes the goals of the humanities from human growth, change, and connection to the traditions of human experience to the collection of more data. The human sciences are about the collection of information, which apparently has no more connection to the self than the information science collects about nature. The type of knowledge one gets when one learns a set of facts about the great philosophers or art history or a series of historical facts does not change the self because it does not demand personal involvement. This is what has made most of modern education so boring and enervating: It is not about experience, but about the accumulation of information. But the information of the humanities, lacking the practical applications of science to controlling nature, has no purpose. If the study of literature, art, and history is not about experiential reorientation, it is not about anything more than mere information. In the human sciences, a theoretical and supposedly value-free wall similar to the sciences is established to control experience.

The irony of the human situation since the evolution of the cerebral cortex and the development of language is that we live within the world as it is, but our knowledge of it is almost always mediated by the presuppositions we have formulated about it. We have become sociolinguistic beings. Language is less (if it is at all) a tool than a medium. The conceptual things we contrive to explain our experiences, the symbols, metaphors, words, sentences, and formulae, are not the things themselves, but representations of things. The experience of the words, symbols, and concepts in both the sciences and the humanities defines a world as it creates a world. But the truths of the words and symbols, although creating worlds, are concomitantly distancing us from the world. It can, of course, be argued, as George Steiner has done, that behind every word, symbol, or sculpture is always a divine other, that even though words are just words, notes just notes, paint just pigments, they denote in themselves, "real presence."[20] There is truth here: The experience one gets in the world of discourse, lets say of Dante, Rilke, or Descartes, of a great scientific or mathematical theory and the like, has a "presence" about it. Dwelling within language is a dwelling within worlds. Here we are talking about the difference between social, scientific, or philosophical information and experience. If we experience a work of literature, say a poem or a novel, we move with language. If we do not move with the language, if we do not have an experience within the language, we have, at best, more information. The diversity of the human experience of reality certainly has something to do with the truths of the experience gained in the realm of discourse. We are not, as modern linguistic philosophy would have it, made poorer by our concepts, our language, but made richer by it. Learn a new scientific concept and your vision of the world is broadened; dwell within Plato's mode of thinking and you acquire another sense of how humans have made sense of their sociocultural reality.

Nevertheless, the problem in both the scientific and the humanistic realm of experience is a loss of the immediacy of the self to the other. The elevation of the conceptual as the mediator of experience certainly yields objective truths in science and personal, albeit sociolinguistically conditioned, truths in the humanities. But if these are the limits of human experience, the linguistic and the mental figures too predominately. Even Bertrand Russell, a man who epitomized the abstract and who never had a religious experience, noted seventy years ago that intuition diminishes as civilization increases.[21] Reading about trout fishing, eating, or sex is one thing, participating in them is another. If, in the process of hitting a baseball or making love, you start conceptualizing (thinking) about doing so, the experience you have is different than the one you were having.

A mystical or religious experience comes down to this: a pure experience untainted by thinking, an unschematized schematic experience of things. The sun continues to set despite Copernicus. Indeed, we relate to other humans, not to chemical reactions called Bill or Mary. Thus, by default, we almost always see things through the concepts we have about them. And while it is true that rationally organizing those concepts frees us from the evidence of our senses, this is not a refutation of the natural appearances of things. Nor is it a refutation of our natural experience with things.[22] Experience is not always tied to the conceptual; the existential contingencies of life always impose themselves on us and push our understanding away from theoretical and linguistically based modes of knowing. This is what snow storms, making love, fly-fishing, hiking, sailing, skiing—you name it—are all about.

Moreover, there is a side of the human being that is fundamentally opposed to a rationalizing, calculating, goal-oriented control of nature. Humans want more than the pragmatic truths that will help them advance in society; they want connections where abstractions offer separation, they seek enhancement of the self's relationship to world. We need and want to stop our mental manipulations of reality. Lawrence was right, "we should find reality in darkness and not in the light of concept." Despite fears over losing control, the human spirit wants to enter into this mysterious universe; there is a desire within us that seeks the mystery at the root of all knowing, that seeks out art and spirit as a source of change and human growth (Steiner), and recognizes in them a different form of knowing. There is in us something that seeks the eternal flux at the source of being as an explanation of being (Heraclitus), that seeks an immediate existential experience with reality unmediated by historically developed cognition (Böhme), that seeks the primeval chaos as and at the source of reality and truth (Wittgenstein). The desire for an understanding of the eternal truths of being, of nature, do occasionally push themselves through the concepts we have developed to control experience. When this happens, an entirely different experience of reality occurs.

The development of the conceptual originated with our ancestors as immediate existential experience was formulated into symbols. Indeed, the formulation of experience into concepts was the precondition for the development of our contemporary conceptual orientation. But primitive peoples at the gap just prior to the development of the conceptual had nonconceptually mediated experience. The development of our conceptual powers contributed to redefining, or better said, the defining of our experiences. Conceptual thinking provided the possibility of understanding and controlling our experiences, but conceptual thinking also initiated a separation from immediate experience. Does this mean that such a development severs all subsequent immediate connections to the direct experience of the other? I think not. Language is not, as Wittgenstein argued, a cage. A mystical experience is an immediate ontic relationship of self to other, a feeling of the connection of being to being. This might have been at one time a natural condition of humankind. Are not all original religious experiences primal or something altogether different? Do we not distinguish between the religious and religion? Can feelings ever be a lie? Or, is it in our conceptually determined interpretation of things that deception occurs? Granted, according to the modern metaphysic it is illogical to assume that such experiences are possible. But suppose you drop the metaphysic? The possibility of having such a mystical experience would rest on dissolving the concepts determining ordinary experience, so that one existed directly within the world, in an unscripted relationship with nature: hence, once again, fly-fishing, hugging children, or taking a walk. And therefore, a mystical experience is really a reclaiming of the instinctual source of life, a reclaiming of the great flow of life itself, a reclaiming of the mystery of our own existence pointing to the mystery of the Other.

Hans Peter Duerr has shown that primitive people recognized the hook of their own civilization and tried to free themselves from it through initiation rituals. Going into the wilderness was not just a training exercise for adulthood but a breakdown of personal scripts and a coming face to face with pure being, pure nature. At that point, they sever the boundary between civilization and wilderness and step into nature.[23] The result was a development of consciousness through an experience with preconceptual nature, a sensing (experiencing) without thought. Such understandings are possible only when civilized (conceptual) experience breaks down. Archaic people and others let their "animal" out by bringing about a lowering of the mental level. At such a point, they came directly to the world. Not the world as a concept, an assumption, thesis, or hypothesis, but the world as an experience the concept tries to define. It is, as Wittgenstein said, everything that is the case. It is, as Böhme would say, everything that is being.

The experience of unscripted experience has been well documented throughout human history and called many things: willessness, mystical, meditative, and contemplative experience. What is common about such experiences is that they are initiated by willful (sometimes the not-willing occurs accidentally) attempts to not will. Quieting the mental allows a direct attention to the immediate experiences of self and events of the moment. Breaking through conceptual scripts gives an unfiltered experience. What one experiences in such situations is the unscripted self, the unscripted other, and the relationships between them. This is a timeless reality, a world without exactness, without a predetermined purpose, without a determined cause, and without a specific goal beyond the process of life: Here, to quote Musil, "good and evil simply fall away, without any pretense of superiority, and in place of all these relations enters a secret rising and ebbing of our being with that of things and other people."[24]

Many people who have had mystical experiences try to give words to that wordless feeling that has become theirs. This is a difficult task and the effort is only a hint or a pointer toward the sublime, the beautiful, the eternal. If we stick to the words, the concept, the idea, the theory, or the metaphysic, we lose connection with that which makes life meaningful. In this sense all religions, sciences, metaphysics, and morals are impertinent: the mental and the abstract, aiming to contrive and control experience, impose a value on something that has no value and can only be appreciated from feeling. The concept is cheap and merely pragmatic; people do not choose to go on living for rational reasons. Unfortunately, as we live in a normal manner within our concepts, we become more and more abstracting, more and more abstract, more and more alienated. A mystical experience is not a dive into insanity; it is not, except perhaps in its intensity, an unusual condition. It is simply a reclaiming of the instinctual source of life, an intuitive realization of our relationships with things.

Such is the point of departure for understanding mysticism. For example, over a twelve-year period, Böhme had a series of conceptual breaks, mystical experiences, or revelations—call them what you will—about Eternal Nature. They were given to him, he claimed, by God. Thus, Böhme claimed that his ideas were not the result of rationally working out the insights of his predecessors. His understanding of creation was through "no work of his own," but rather the result of a series of illuminations he was "given" during moments when he quieted the rational patterns of his mind and paid close attention to the moment. Böhme's efforts at understanding were first directed towards what Philip Novak has described as the "cultivation of sustained, observational, nonreactive attention to inner and outer experience," exclusive of the "flotsam of ordinary thinking."[25] During a mystical experience, the mystic pays attention to the nondiscursive aspects of his consciousness, not to the continual patterns of thought the rational mind normally concerns itself with. Böhme claimed that these experiences gave him an understanding of the physical forces precipitating life; his books, the experience conceptualized, were descriptions of the physics of matter and the origins of the universe.

Chapter 3

Mystical Experiences

> In modern times the individual finds the abstract form ready-made; the effort to grasp and appropriate it is more the direct driving-forth of what is within and the truncated generation of the universal than it is the emergence of the latter from the concrete variety of existence. Hence the task nowadays consists not so much in purging the individual of an immediate, sensuous mode of apprehension . . . rather in just the opposite, in freeing determinate thoughts from their fixity so as to give actuality to the universal, and impart to it spiritual life.
>
> G.W.F. Hegel

Feeling, not thought, is primary. An individual who has a mystical experience makes an epistemological claim that contradicts ordinary views of how we acquire knowledge. Mystics claim that they have had an experience that has no relation to the thoughts or experiences of their normal life. They also add that those experiences have given them a knowledge of reality distinct from the conceptually based, rationally developed knowledge of the sciences. As opposed to the rational, discursive, or analytical mode of knowing, the mystical event is recognized as an immediate, illuminative experience that provides a knowledge of reality not available through cognitive efforts. As such, a mystical experience is an existential event, experienced more as a feeling than a state of intellect; however, the event is not only a state of feeling but a state of knowledge.[1] As with sense experience, it has an origin outside the self, but the experience is not similar to normal everyday seeing, hearing, smelling, and touching. Rather, despite the fact that what one experiences is precipitated by something outside the self, an intuitive sense or understanding occurs; during a mystical, experience one experiences and understands something but one does not simply see or hear something. Additionally, although something becomes known during a mystical experience, what becomes known is not the result of a rational assessment of things, of putting things together. A sense of something in the form of an insight, vision, or illumination occurs to the individual. This sudden uncontrived (from rational precepts) glimpse of things provides an understanding of Eternal Nature.

The results of this experience (i.e., the knowledge gained from the mystical event) are difficult to fully describe, although, as we shall see, Böhme wrote volumes about what he experienced. The French philosopher and mathematician Blaise Pascal wrote his experiences down in a poem.

> From about half past ten in the evening to
> about half an hour after midnight.
> Fire.
> God of Abraham, God of Isaac, God of Jacob,
> Not the God of philosophers and scholars.
> Absolute Certainty: Beyond reason.
> Joy. Peace.
> Forgetfulness of the world and everything
> but God.
> The World has not known thee,
> but I have known thee.
> Joy! joy! joy! tears of joy!

Pascal's poem suggests the nature of the experience many people have had during and immediately following a mystical experience: a feeling of unity or wholeness and peace, a perception that the universe, ourselves, and all things in it are part of a system that is working perfectly. During and after a mystical experience the plurality of our normal perceptions and the sense of difference that we experience are recognized as illusory. Some individuals claim that their intuitive vision reveals that good and evil are nonexistent and that time does not exist. Böhme claimed, seemingly contradicting these more common assertions, that during his mystical experiences, good and evil as well as time were an absolute part of the universe. Despite this darker vision of reality, Böhme was at peace with his vision; the world was as it was because it had to be. This was, as Leibniz said, the best of all possible worlds. All mystical experiences cut through the rational-historical experiences of the individual. Mystical experiences themselves are not tied to time, place, or mental structures, nor are they the result of rationally working out a new knowledge from a historically established position.

Herein lies the issue of mysticism. Is it possible for an individual to escape, even for a moment, historical conditioning? Can there truly be a knowledge that is not the result of an evolution of the thoughts and ideas humans have acquired over time? Are mystical experiences an existential possibility for a species whose evolutionary achievement has been the development of rational consciousness? In our specific case, did Böhme have the revelations he claimed or was the knowledge he expressed merely an elaboration on his historically developed and derived knowledge, a fact that he conveniently forgot? A most important question arises if these questions are answered affirmatively: What are the factors and conditions within the self that allow for such an experience?

One final point: If it is possible that a mystical experience transcends historical prejudices and mentally derived patterns of thought, if this form of understanding is not the result of adding to the concatenation of historically constructed knowledge, what is that knowledge? What does anyone who has a mystical experience come to understand about the world? What is understood when one understands outside of the mental realms of understanding we have rationally constructed in language? What does one know when one knows prior to or beyond self-reflective thought?

Thus, if our mental orientations to events determine our experiences of things—and mystics claim that their understanding is derived from a source outside their thought processes—what is the nature of that experience, what are the factors in the self that permit this knowledge and what is the knowledge acquired from a mystical experience? In this chapter, I discuss points one and two. What Böhme learned during his mystical experience is taken up in chapter six.

The Nature of Mystical Experiences

Can we talk about experience that leads to knowledge that does not have an original mental component? Since all of us have had nonlinguistically based understandings about things at one time or another, and indeed, since most of us seek out experiences that might provide us with a knowledge that goes beyond our historically conditioned truth about things, most of us have experienced the ontic state of the mystic. We all sense the need to experience and understand the world from a nonpragmatic, nonrational position; all the meditative-like activities we participate in—gardening, listening to music, fishing, hiking, swimming, looking at mountains, and the like—are enjoyed, I believe, because they have an effect on the self that is similar to a mystical experience. When done without contrivance, they can become meditatively involving activities and experiences that reunite us with ourselves by reconnecting us with the rhythms of nature. The peace we feel after several days in the woods and the dishevelment on reentering a city is a common experience. The fly-fisherman Lee Wulff claimed that he could feel the heartbeat of the salmon he was playing, but I suspect that all of us when we go into nature are trying to "re-merge" ontically with some form of eternal heartbeat. And making love (perhaps the most obvious example of an orientation to things different than the normal condition of rational control) is not the way that we commonly perceive it—merely a survival oriented and generated activity. Something ontic occurs while gardening, fly-fishing, skiing, and the like that involves unity and connection to the other, or even to the Other.

There is nothing really mysterious about this, it is simply a primal feeling state, our bodies' relationships to things; this is an autochthonic connection to being, and it is necessary if wholeness and balance is to be achieved in one's life. Our bodies are always feeling such states, but during our hectic, pragmatically driven activities, we fail to allow ourselves to pay attention to them. The rhythmic activity of gardening or whatever, puts the pragmatic goals that one has on hold, so to speak, and one becomes more attuned to different relationship to the world. Such experiences provide people with a sense of what life is on a level different than that provided in our pragmatic orientation to things. True, the activity and the ontic conditions that provide for its possibility do not offer a knowledge that we can manipulate and control for immediate advancement in the world: You do not earn a living in a meditative state. But this sense of being in the world when the world is not simply for our use is important. It provides us with an ahistorical, nonrationally mediated sense of being with things. It also helps us comprehend what is happening during a mystical experience and what it is that mystics come to understand about the world.

Such a knowledge and the orientation that makes it possible is revealed, as Martha Heyneman pointed out, in the paintings on the walls of the caves at Altamira. "Those artists were not painting the bison as we would see it—as a great mountain of meat out there," a standing reserve for use. They were "painting the bison that was inside them. They had taken the bison into themselves, as the Zen archer takes in the target."[2] The body-sense of the external world, unfettered by socially contrived and pragmatically developed concepts of things, allows the individual to begin to share in the "underlying life of the ultimately real."[3] This is a primordial experience; the somatosensory experience of things unconfined by the higher order mental structures the human species has evolved in its history and through language. In such a condition one feels and comes to know about life and death, the soul and God. As I noted in the previous chapter, Musil described this as an engagement in "a secret rising and ebbing of our being with that of things and other people." Böhme described his experiences as an inner understanding of Eternal Nature. The salient points of his writings are descriptions of his revelatory experience, that is, Eternal Nature. "I saw and knew the essence of all essences, the ground and the unground . . . the causes and primal condition of this world, and all creatures."[4]

According to Böhme and his historical predecessors, mystical experience and the knowledge it provides have to do with involvement with life on a plane of inner connection to outer experience. If these inner experiences have something to do with a relationship to things and if they are more than a chemical imbalance or a synoptic misfiring, or, as one dour critic put it, the form of error that mistakes for a divine manifestation operations of the merely human faculty, mystical knowledge must result when two interrelated conditions are met. The first is when individuals for some reason subvert or stop or have stopped the process of organizing the images the body receives according to preformed sociolinguistic symbols. This, it might be added, is what all Christian, Jewish, and Muslim prayer practices as well as the traditions that arose in India (viz., Hinduism and Buddhism) are designed to accomplish. The goal is to stop mental chatter and to "release the human being from the bondage to the machinations of [the] false self." To starve one's thoughts in order to "re-collect the ontic freedom and clarity that are [our] birthright."[5] The mental organization of things is not brought into immediate use. In conjunction with this, a cessation of the pragmatic functioning of our mental orientation (the part that has allowed us to evolve as a species and individually—the builders of bridges, careers, airplanes, etc.)—must occur. The part of the human brain concerned with organizing experience to ensure the advancement of the self and species, guiding experience with particular ends in mind, is not in command during a mystical event. Let me elaborate.

Current neurological theories divide the brain into an older brain core, responsible for the basic biological regulation of the organism, and the more recently evolved neocortex. "Upstairs in the cortex there is reason and will power, while downstairs in the subcortex there is emotion and all that weak, fleshy stuff."[6] These older areas of the brain are in charge of monitoring the state of the body as it functions internally and in connection to the world. The newer upper areas are where consciousness and rationality transpire. But reasoning does not work without the biological regulation of the subcortical brain stem— this is an interactive system.

The process of consciousness that has enabled humans to dominate the world involves the following sequence of events. An event occurs, we feel something, the lower levels of the brain take notice.[7] An image is formed. The upper regions of the brain can then become involved. If the upper regions become involved, they do so from the conscious perspective the individual has evolved in the course of his or her life. Damasio calls the responses that take place in consciousness "acquired dispositional representations." Acquired dispositional representations come about after an event occurs and the brain pairs the event with certain "emotional responses in [the] individual's experience." The individual's unique experiences, the learned responses to events, color the new event and create not a primary but a secondarily induced representation in the brain. Consciousness and rationality result when the sensations or feelings are experienced as images and then filtered into the frameworks we have developed over time and past experience becoming particular concepts.

The ordering of the symbols, words, and language we have adopted to represent the image is the process called thought. Thought, as with consciousness, evolves when our concepts are changed over time.[8] "What is happening to us now is, in fact, happening to a concept of self based on the past, including the past that was current only a moment ago."[9] Consequently, not only are there differences between feelings (emotions) and the concepts but also between the primary experiences of the body and the secondary or acquired emotional responses to the image that have evolved in consciousness. One is an ontic, the other a mental event. "The early body signals, in both evolution and development, helped form a 'basic concept' of the self; this basic concept provided the ground reference for whatever else happened to the organism."[10] The evolution of mental experience over ontic experience is the source of our strength: We can control our perceptions and build on our world. The source of our weakness, or, better put, the source of our imbalance is that in a world of inner and outer ontic activity, we abstract and lose touch with the immediate experiences of the body. We live our lives from within the constructed concept of self. As Damasio puts it, "language may not be the source of the self, but it certainly is the source of the 'I.' "[11]

The process of abstracting from the body's immediate experience of things through acquired dispositional representations forms the basis of pragmatic, rational responses to life. It enables us to overcome the chaos and immediacy of events and order them to our benefit. Consciousness takes place within our acquired dispositional representations. Since this is where most of us do our living, our experiencing, the dominant characteristic of human experience, has become less the feeling, less the immediate relationship and primal image and more the concept: Normal consciousness has become a concept organized through the symbolic linguistic traditions of which we are a part. But the original source of what became our concepts remains—the body's sense of itself and its relationship to the outer world as experienced and assessed by the lower cortical regions of the brain. We simply do not pay attention to them anymore.

Hegel was making this point in the opening quotation to this chapter. The abstract is now ready-made. We are raised in an abstract world and away from the immediate concrete experience of things. In moving away from immediate experience, we have gained control of the world but clouded our sense of the universal and the spiritual. Thus, Hegel's point is that the object today is to free "determinate thoughts from their fixity so as to give actuality to the universal, and [thereby] impart to it a spiritual life." If the mind is always geared to a pragmatic agenda, it will fail to fully register the nonpragmatic sense of things, the sense of God or art. James tied an appreciation of the arts to the susceptibility of mystical experience: "We are alive or dead to the eternal inner message of the arts according as we have kept or lost this mystical susceptibility."[12] No one smells the roses if they are always building bridges. Arthur Deikman comes to a similar conclusion. In a series of experiments, subjects were asked to meditate on a vase. Mystical connections occurred. Deikman suggested that this was the result of a "de-automatization of the psychological structures that organize, limit, select, and interpret perceptual stimuli.... De-automatization is an undoing of the automatizations of apparatuses—both means and goal structures—directed toward the environment."[13] To Deikman, it is "more accurate to say that the undoing of automatic perceptual and cognitive structures permits a gain in sensory intensity and richness at the expense of abstract categorization and differentiation."[14]

A mystical experience might therefore take place as follows: An ontic connection to an event occurs, it is understood in a fundamental way by the subcortical regions of the brain, and it is left unfettered by any instantaneous response by consciousness. The important step is the last one. During mystical experiences the individual is experiencing feeling relationships with things in the nonrational, nonpragmatic parts of the brain and the theoretical constructs contained within the neocortex do not, for whatever reason, overshadow the experience with historically constructed interpretation. Mental image does not subsume felt experience.

In contrast to the normal, everyday conscious orientation to reality, the mystic strives for openness to raw events, such as the self's relationship to the other. The environmentally adaptive behavior that a functioning individual uses to maintain and advance itself in the world ceases and the individual stands in a more or less somatosensory way before things. This permits ontic connection. What one gets during such moments is more a felt-experience of things and less a mental interpretation of things. The mystical state might relate to what Damasio calls the "background feeling" of the body—the body's sense of being in the world. He described this state as corresponding to a "body state prevailing between emotions" and giving an individual a "sense of being, a feeling of life itself." In this state, the most primal level of feeling is represented.[15] What Damasio fails to explain is that this body state must also be intimately connected with the external world, that there is on this level of experience an intimate connection and relationship between the self and the other. Put yourself into or drift into a meditative state and you begin to experience things less as a thought and more as a somatosensory connection. The background feeling must certainly be traced back to our one-cell ancestors and their body state in the environment.

During a mystical experience, a person is living less within the neural representations of things called to mind as one or another symbolic representation that help it advance in the world and more within the immediate sensation of things. The mental screens we have used to navigate our way through the world are dropped. All such experiences offer a knowledge, one that connects and unites, one that is always available to us, but because of our absorption in the linguistic representation of things developed in our personal history and in our practical organization of all information, such experiences are hidden from our view. Now, what about Böhme?

Factors Permitting Mystical Experiences

I have already spoken about the historical and topical forces that shaped Böhme's view of things and about his sensitive and reflective personality. He was a man of his times, unsettled by new scientific theories that had thrown the world and God out of joint and disturbed that things went as well for the evil as the good (what was God doing?). He was cognizant of the antinomies and contradictions of everyday life and felt doomed by the thought that life had no meaning, no future, and no substance beyond the here and now. Stuck within the prejudices, biases, and idols of his mind and time and stuck within his mental screens (the theoretical determining his experiences), Böhme had the good fortune to have a mystical experience, then another, and another and another. The first one occurred in 1600, the last in 1612.

I do not think that his mystical experiences, except perhaps in terms of intensity and frequency, were much different than those thousands of other people have spoken about. Certainly, having a mystical experience is remarkable event; they occur to very few people and not very frequently. Nevertheless, there is a long and well-documented history of mystical experiences. Many individuals prior to and after Böhme have had them, and Böhme's were similar to all the others. The mystical experience cut through his mental screens, the theoretically controlled and manipulated views that determined prior experiences. The mystical event washed Böhme's screens away—for the moment—and presented him with a raw experience, a raw, nonfiltered, pretheoretical experience. During his mystical experience, Böhme was engaged with reality at some somatosensory level of his being. This was a felt-experience, not a mentally judged experience. "I was raised up in God . . . and my sadness disappeared. In this light my spirit had quickly seen through everything."[16] The cerebral parts of his brain—the area of the brain that provides us with reason, calculation, and the ability to plan and control reality, the part of the brain that enabled humans to be useful and organize what we experience in such a way that we can turn it to our advantage—were on hold. Böhme was not thinking, planning, calculating, moaning, or worrying about one thing or another, he was simply a sensing organism sensing without critical thought. He was touched, as he said, in his spirit. That is my first point.

The second point I want to make is about the knowledge one receives during such moments. If it is true that during such experiences, the compulsive, calculative, controlling, manipulative, contriving state in which we normally exist stops, then a deepening of the person's ontological relationships occurs. The unscreened somatosensory experience results in a form of ontological knowledge. When the mental is turned off (in this case, cut off), one is being (sensing) differently on some level than when one is being in terms of the useful, pragmatic consciousness. The knowledge one acquires during such moments has to do with some biological relationship of self to other, some somatic knowledge unfiltered by higher level, historically conditioned and developed theoretical prejudices. I think that it is in such states that people have religious experiences, experience God, or touch reality in a different way. Böhme called what he experienced an inner experience and he characterized the knowledge he received as an inner knowledge.

The last point I want to make about Böhme's mystical experience is that he was not given the particulars of the things he wrote about (creation, evolution, and God's role in things) during his mystical experience. Whereas the intensity of the experience was great, the exactness of the understanding was not. These were visions, felt-senses of the origins and interrelations of things. His knowledge, the sense of things his visions provoked, did not stay with him but continued to come to him from "time to time," so that he "circled around it for twelve years."[17] The experience was not some complex step by step outline that detailed exactly how the universe was put together and therefore he was not able to simply transcribe the experience onto paper. "Because I could not grab ahold of the deep birth of God, and comprehend it in my reason I had to seek for twelve more years before truth was given to me."[18] What he received during his mystical experiences was more an intense sense of things, an overarching vision of unity grounded in God. Mystical knowledge, although intense, may be overwhelming as an experience (especially compared to our normal state of being) but it is intense sensation, not intense thought. What he did over the twelve years was make effort after effort to rationally describe what he had witnessed. This accounts for the scattered, redundant, discombobulated nature of his first book. It was effort after effort to rationally organize a mystical experience.

Given this, what makes Böhme remarkable and marks his achievement is that following his revelations, he took the felt-experiences (the inner knowledge) and developed an explanation of how creation began, how the universe worked and evolved, and how the divine being was a part but not responsible for the entirety of events occurring in the universe. This was the cerebral mind taking the noncerebral experience and putting it into language. His achievement entailed taking this sense of the unity, wholeness, and interconnectedness of things and drawing a grand encompassing picture of the universe. Böhme's achievement was not his revelation (that was a gift) but the offering, from his vision, of an explanation of how the universe is put together and works. His explanations, worked out over a twenty-year period (after 1612, he kept trying to describe his understandings) and in many different books, were an attempt to put into comprehensive form the sense of things he acquired during his intuitions. His books were an attempt to articulate how things are from an inner, raw perspective.

Let us be clear here. In seeking to take the vision he had about the universe and God and offer an explanation of how everything tied together, Böhme moved from the felt-experience of things (the pretheoretical) into the theoretical. Böhme's books are the felt-knowledge conceptualized and applied to the problem of explaining creation, cosmology, and nature. In these definitions and descriptions, Böhme incorporated the sociolinguistic structures available to him — his language, metaphors, and analogies were all one with his times. The description and articulation of his intuition was in time; the source from which it sprung and the knowledge was outside time. Despite the vocabulary, rooted in his sociohistorical context, Böhme's explanation sought to present a picture of the world as it worked from an understanding born out of time.

There are two important issues that arise from this and they are taken up in the next two chapters: We need to explain and elaborate the particulars of Böhme's attempt to rationally describe how the universe worked from the felt-sense he acquired during his mystical experiences. What did Böhme say about God, creation, and nature? In the next chapter I will discuss the ontological understanding Böhme acquired. If Böhme's knowledge was born from a source outside time, what does that knowledge have to do with human beings? Is there any value and validity to mystical understanding, and if so what is it? What does this intuitive felt-experience of things, called a mystical experience, mean?

CHAPTER 4

ALCHEMY AND THE INNER KNOWLEDGE OF NATURE

> There is nothing more difficult for a truly creative painter than to paint a rose, because before he can do so he must forget all the roses that were ever painted.
>
> Henri Matisse

> If only we could pull out our brain and use only our eyes.
>
> Pablo Picasso

The point of the first three chapters was to put the issue of mystical experience and inner intuitive knowledge into sharper focus. I described the dialectical character of experience, the bouncing back and forth between our conceptual orientation packages and the events that occur to us to show that most of our experiences and most of our claims to knowledge take place within a historical and linguistic framework. In developing the distinctions between the patterns of thought that govern perspectives within the sciences and the humanities (everyday speech), I want to illustrate how the traditions of each help to determine a reality. Individuals in the sciences and the humanities and all of us in our sociocultural orientations are normally in a dialogue within a particular set of assumptions conditioned by the language we learn in our social environment or have been trained in. We acquire a "view"; the view determines an orientation to the world, and this orientation is primarily a mental one. Such we call our conscious mind.

I also want to show that our mental orientations to things dominate our consciousness. Our ancestors were culturally Greco-Roman, yet we have inherited the outer courtyard and lost the inner one. We look at nature as things over there that we can measure. These measurements provide us with the only true knowledge we can have about things. We relate with ourselves and we interrelate with others within a noetic medium designed to give us an objective knowledge of nature. To know today is to think impersonally, to be detached. Thus, knowledge is mediated memory and thought is the response of that memory. Nietzsche's statement that "rational thought is interpretation according to a scheme which we cannot escape," has validity insofar as we remain within our metaphysical screens.[1]

Most of our experiences with things, conditioned by our assumptions, are not new, they are conditional and additional. The intellect is a practical faculty that evolved and insured our biological success, but as our mental powers developed the conceptual came to override experience. Most of our lives are spent living within a collective, linguistic-sensory delusion. Our rationally evolved patterns of thought can change, but it requires an event inspiring or shocking enough to force a reconsideration of our assumptions. Snow storms might alter our orientations because they can cut through our assumptions about things and possibly open us up to a new experience.[2] I tie the purely existential, unscripted experience of snow storms into the basic mystical experience. A mystical experience provides an inner knowledge of reality; it is not for use, but it is ontically compelling.

This chapter and the next have a dual purpose. On the one hand I will discuss the two historical traditions that shaped Böhme's life, showing how he was tied to the sociointellectual traditions of his time. In this sense I will be developing a context for understanding his mystical experiences. The two traditions of thought that Böhme absorbed during his formative years were the occult/alchemical views of Paracelsus and his followers and the spiritualist views of Caspar Schwenckfeld and his followers. I will examine the epistemologies of sixteenth century alchemy and spiritualism and their subsequent ontological implications. For Böhme, the alchemical and spiritualist traditions established the foundation on which his mystical experiences were built, they set up the possibility of his having mystical experiences and of breaking from those traditions. Although it is certainly not necessary to train for a mystical experience, a developed or natural predisposition toward their possibility seems required. Böhme was educated towards receiving a mystical experience because he was part of two philosophical traditions that stressed the value of inner modes of knowledge.

The sixteenth century was a breakthrough period for alchemists and spiritualists. Separating themselves from the epistemological strictures of the Catholic Church and subsequently the Lutheran Church, they reopened ancient Gnostic ideas on an intuitive inner knowing born from a participatory existential relationship with things. Were their ideas a continuation of the aberrant ideas of the occult past? A bad set of ideas waiting to be replaced by the rational and objective epistemology of modern science?

Derivative Knowledge/Intuitive Knowledge

Inner modes of knowing such as those practiced by various monastic and contemplative groups have always been a part of the Western religious tradition. Usually they were a thorn in the side of the dominant, rationally governed power structures or correctives to a hardening theology or ideology.[3]

For the priest or rabbi, whose primary duty is to convey doctrine, it is always difficult to have a saint or a mystic in the parish. The one believes truth is a doctrine, the other an experience and intuitive insight. The one validates the conceptual, the other the intuitive personal. In the sixteenth century, perhaps in response to the liberating nature of the Renaissance and the Reformation, the occult and the spiritualist traditions experienced their own renaissance. Occult philosophers like Paracelsus, on a track that would later be followed by Galileo, led an assault on what its practitioners believed were stagnant theories of knowledge and tradition-bound educational practices of contemporary university systems. Spiritualists like Schwenckfeld questioned the rigidity of Protestant religious doctrine. Both were concerned with advancing an inner mode of knowing, a mode of knowing distinct from the conceptually governed critical and impersonal knowing of the theologians. Does the person who knows the doctrine best have a monopoly on truth? Paracelsus and Schwenckfeld answered, "definitely not."

Böhme, the seventeenth century heir to both confirmed and advanced the inner epistemological position originally generated by the most famous sixteenth century occultists and spiritualists. If Böhme had had his way, the values of the modern world would have included not simply the epistemological and metaphysical values of science but, complementing those and establishing the importance of intuitive forms of understanding, the occult and spiritualist epistemological values as well.

Böhme wanted to establish the importance of an inner intuitive knowledge of the world, but he was not opposed to the advancement of what he called an outer (rational) knowledge to understand and say something about reality. Although an inner knowledge of reality was a commonly recognized epistemological possibility, acquiring an inner knowledge of reality was always recognized (even at that time) as something that occurred rarely. When it did, it conferred great status on an individual.[4] The reputation that Böhme acquired during his life and the fame that is still accorded him is based on his claim that all his knowledge was inner knowledge; everything that he knew was a result of a series of revelatory experiences that had nothing to do with his historical or rational knowledge.

Hegel's positioning of Böhme alongside Bacon as the other great father of modern philosophy has merit because it juxtaposes inner epistemological values against outer epistemological values—the conceptual versus the intuitive. Paracelsus, Böhme, Hegel, Blake, and Lawrence honor inner knowledge; the English and French philosophical position, articulated by Bacon and developed during the Enlightenment, grounds truth in the concept. The concept provides distance and the possibility of the detached observation necessary if objective knowledge is to occur because the concept is within a particular intellectual screen. Böhme's inner intuitive knowledge, which is not grounded in the concept, is belittled as subjective, as a personal bias.

This, therefore, is the issue of Böhme: Is it possible to acquire a knowledge of the origins of the universe and workings of nature intuitively? Did Böhme really have these revelatory (mystical) experiences and intuitively receive the knowledge he claimed? Did he really receive an inner understanding of Eternal Nature?

There are three possible answers. The first is that Böhme, continuing an old debate, did not have the intuitions he claimed he did; he was simply synthesizing historical and contemporary ideas. That is, that all Böhme's knowledge was, like everybody else's knowledge, derivative. The second is that Böhme's statements were the ravings of a slightly insane man with equally unstable followers. The third is that his statements and claims have validity, that his knowledge was "not from reason's work" as he was wont to say, but from a "superior source." If this is the case, then Böhme's statements are an example of a vision and understanding of the universe derived from a source different from that which results from a pragmatically driven, rationally organized orientation to things. I am assuming in what follows that there is some truth to Böhme's claims, not that it is superior to the knowledge gained by the scientific investigation of nature, just that it is different. Let me briefly discuss each of these possibilities.

The possibility that Böhme's statements were derivative, showing obvious historical connections to contemporary thought, and were, like all other human utterances, socioculturally determined, is compelling. There is truth here. Böhme's writings do borrow from the context of the time and can be recognized as a response to several interrelated social conflicts. The first of these conflicts is similar to the dispute illustrated by Carlo Ginzberg in his book, *The Cheese and the Worms*.[5] Ginzberg draws out the antagonisms between the knowledge claims of the upper (superior) and the lower (inferior) classes. As a largely uneducated shoemaker, Böhme would seem to be clearly aligned to one class rather than another. But most of his friends were from the aristocratic classes, and it was the wealthier, better educated aristocrats who encouraged Böhme to write, advanced distribution and discussion of his works, and financially supported his family. Moreover, social critique never appeared to be a serious issue for Böhme. In his letters, his essays, and books, we do not discover attacks on the aristocratic classes or even significant social concerns.

A second possibility for the derivative nature of Böhme's knowledge is that he was involved in the fundamental Lutheran epistemological conflict between the spiritually enlightened individual and the Biblically learned individual. We might reduce this conflict to the battle between the theologian and the mystic, the word versus the spirit, the learned individual versus the spiritually enlightened individual. In the Lutheran tradition, the issue goes back to the dialogues Schwenckfeld had with Luther. Was true Christian understanding merely a matter of reading the Bible, eating the bread, and drinking the wine or did it not take some type of spiritual awakening for such external things to become meaningful? After the *Formula of Concord* solidified the structure of Lutheran belief in 1577, the clash between the rational dogmatism of the Lutheran hierarchy who upheld an absolute reading of the Bible and the more spiritually oriented Lutherans expanded. During the latter part of the sixteenth century, the more spiritually inclined Lutherans formed clandestine religious societies.[6] These societies were study groups and Böhme belonged to one of them. The historical factors of this tradition and their effect on Böhme's epistemological position are discussed in the next chapter.

Finally, it is possible that Böhme was engaged in and influenced by the ongoing battle between outsider occult philosophy and insider university philosophy—an educated scholar/uneducated layman battle.

Since Paracelsus's debates with the professors in the early sixteenth century, a conflict had been waged between the rather rigid tradition-bound university philosophers and the occult philosophers. According to the occult philosophers, the problem with the science of the university philosophers was their adherence to a fixed corpus, their stress on rationality as the means to knowledge, and their unwillingness to go into the field and actually perform physical investigations of nature. Böhme was clearly influenced by the occult philosophy of the sixteenth century—Paracelsus was one of his "great masters"— and the question of superior occult knowledge as opposed to inferior university knowledge is certainly a historically conditioned aspect of Böhme's writings. The traditions of occult philosophy (especially Paracelsus) and their influence on Böhme cannot be denied.

Nevertheless, despite the historical factors that influenced Böhme, it is also possible that he had the revelations he said he did and that what he experienced was not conditioned by his intellectual heritage. While Böhme was involved in and influenced by the spirit/book debates of Lutheranism and the scholar/laymen debates of sixteenth century occult philosophy, something of what he came to know, I believe, was from revelation. History and the intellectual atmosphere of early seventeenth century Görlitz set up the possibility for Böhme's mystical experiences but did not determine its content. Böhme was indeed part of an ongoing scholar/laymen epistemological battle, and he was involved in and influenced by the radical Lutheran spiritualist conflict with the Church hierarchy, but what he derived from these two traditions were epistemological and anthropological beliefs. These established his ontological stand before things, and this stand set up the possibilities for his revelatory experiences. Historical orientation provided the basis for the possibility of revelatory experiences and placed them within a context. However, the experiences themselves were not the result of a pragmatic position before things, nor were they evolved from a calculative or logical approach to things.

Böhme may have lacked a formal education, but he grew up in an environment that provided him with a set of metaphysical assumptions about the nature of reality and the best way to acquire knowledge about it. Perhaps Böhme's most significant assumptions were derived from sixteenth century occult/magical philosophy, especially Paracelsian philosophy.[7] During the last quarter of the sixteenth and first quarter of the seventeenth century, Paracelsus' writings were reprinted and his philosophical ideas revived.[8] Interest in Paracelsus' ideas was widespread during the span of Böhme's life. Indeed, Paracelsian philosophy was a significant part of intellectual matrix of late sixteenth century Görlitz. Several of Böhme's friends were Paracelsians and in the decade preceding his series of revelations (1590-1600), Böhme belonged to a study group led by Möller, a radical Lutheran pastor.[9] Möller expressed the Paracelsian-influenced Christology of Valentine Weigel combined with the radical spiritualism of Schwenckfeld.[10]

The fundamental tenets of Paracelsian philosophy (and of most of the occult philosophy of the sixteenth century) can be divided into two separate if interrelated categories: (1) a Neo-Platonic cosmology that included a separation theory of creation and (2) a Gnostic belief that true and absolute knowledge came as a gift from God. Böhme adopted these assumptions. They were to him what relative space and time or natural selection are to twentieth-century scientists: assumed, unquestioned truths that influenced the questions he asked, the direction of his interests, and the results he sought. There is no doubt that these beliefs guided his experience of things and set up the possibility of his revelations. They did not, however, determine the exact nature of the mystical experiences he had any more than a description of an earthquake can determine one's response to an actual earthquake.

Walter Pagel has already shown that Neo-Platonic cosmological principles lay at the root of all sixteenth and seventeenth century occult activity and, in fact, supplied the "overriding doctrinal basis for the work of Paracelsus."[11] Based on these cosmological theories, sixteenth century natural philosophers made several assumptions. They were inspired by a vision of nature as spiritually alive, interconnected, and springing from the same source. There was a unity and wholeness to all life. "Everything is conserved by one element, namely, by that from which it is sprung,"[12] claimed Paracelsus. All things originate from the "invisible, we are made from the Arcanum," which is "permanent in the ultimate Mysterium Magnum."[13] This Arcanum is that which is "incorporeal, immortal, or perpetual life, intelligible above all nature and of knowledge more than human."[14] Thus, the correspondence between all things was ultimately a connection to the One. The material world, derived from the spiritual world, which in turn emanated from Nous, had evolved from God.

These beliefs enlivened occult philosophy from Paracelsus to Böhme and spurred investigation of nature. Nature was the second book of God, the final out-flowing of the divine; therefore, if you studied nature, you studied (at some remove) God. To the sixteenth century occult philosopher, the quest for knowledge of nature was a desire for a reunion with the original emanation, a climb backwards and upwards on the ladder of evolution to the divine One.

Neo-Platonic cosmology also presented a dualistic conception of nature. Nature was not simply material, it was also spiritual. There was a dual aspect to nature; nature consisted of the soul that had descended from the One and the corporeal body that housed the soul. The "visible sensible things are an essence of the invisible."[15] To Böhme, the spiritual inner aspect of nature was as obvious as the material one we now profess to believe in. If you "look at the material world," he said, "you see a likeness of the Paradisical world. Because the world comes out of the first root, therein do all things stand."[16] To Böhme, the whole outward visible world was "a signature or figure of the inward spiritual world."[17] Both Paracelsus and Böhme maintained that the important aspect of nature was the spiritual part and that the tangible object was an expression of the spiritual core. "The physically visible and the invisible are before human eyes, the one part we should see only as a figured spirit."[18]

As Böhme expressed it, the "earth is the gross out-flowing of this subtle spirit,"[19] a "house, husk and instrument of the inward spiritual world which is hidden therein and works through it."[20] Nature was the "total of the acting invisible spiritual forces that create, form and are active in matter.[21] Nature was not simply the various trees, flowers, dogs, rocks, and the like, it was the inner force of things. The outer form was the expression of an inner force, and it was the inner force of things that had to be understood. Thus, nature was not a system of random bodies interacting in cause and effect relationships in space and time or a system of natural laws ruling bodies. Nature was a constantly dynamic inner force, a complex collection of souls, seeds, and spirits inherent in the matrix of the world and made visible in the living entities we witness around us.

A soul or a psychic force existed in every rock and tree. Nature worked because the souls had imagination and will. They imagine and will themselves forward into corporeal reality. Soul, spirit, will, and mind are the dynamic forces that precipitate the movements and changes of life. What was once the transcendent above was now immanent and animating presence.

Everything was alive with its own special form of living and its own unique expression. Paracelsus himself had witnessed the life of coal when he worked in the mines. The veins of coal started deep in the earth and rose to the surface. The "life of things is none other than a spiritual essence, an invisible and impalpable thing."[22] The life of dung was its smell; when the smell ended, the soul had departed. Rain was the "imbibition of the earth." The life of metals was a "latent fatness which they have received from Sulfur," and the life of Sulfur was a "combustible, ill-smelling fatness."[23]

The life of dung? All this sounds a bit crazy. But the alchemist's sense of a knowing generated from the life of things experienced within, intuitively suggests an existential truth similar to that of primitive peoples and native American Indians. The heart of occult investigations was the dual nature of life—the sense that there was an inner and an outer nature of thing—and that an inner understanding was the only true knowledge. And thus, the "life of dung" was really a statement on the soul's understanding of the eternal life in all things, a statement implying that all things have a place in and an influence on the world.

When alchemists and occult philosophers sought an understanding of the inner essence of things, they were driven by a desire to understand the lived life of things. When occult philosophers grasped that, they made inroads toward understanding what cured disease, started plants growing from small seeds, and made life and kept it going. It is impossible to understand alchemical or occult investigations of nature without realizing that inherently they were a corrective to the rational knowledge of the university. Alchemists claimed that they were teachers of sacred knowledge and that university professors were teachers of profane knowledge. Perhaps, Emerson's words are accurate here too: The distinction between them, like that

> Between poets like Herbert, and poets like Pope; between philosophers like Spinoza, Kant and Coleridge—and philosophers like Locke, Paley, Mackintosh and Stewart; between men of the world who are reckoned accomplished talkers, and here and there a fervent mystic . . . is that one class speak from within, or from experience, as parties and possessors of the fact; and the other class from without, as spectators merely.[24]

Böhme often remarked that he was not trying to deride the external knowledge of nature developed by the sciences of his time but that he simply wanted to balance the epistemological scales. An individual who had no sense of the inner realms of being, an individual who did not acquire his or her knowledge from within the recesses of the self as revelation, an individual whose sense of understanding of life was weighted totally in favor of rational comprehension and practical control was, at best, seeing only half the picture.

The difficulties encountered in knowing something about the world from this position are daunting. Since almost everything in this world was alive, life was a combining, changing, growing, and propagating spiritual force. Speaking metaphorically, in the occult world of the sixteenth century, the linear world of mathematics was not applicable: 1 + 1 was not 2; it was 3 or 5 or 47 or 105. One chicken and one rooster got together and the interesting sum of that engagement to the occult philosopher was not that there were now two birds, but that there would be a dozen; likewise with snakes and maggots. The alchemist experienced the world as dynamic flux, a Heraclitean fire.

The problem of allowing oneself to engage in a world of constant spiritual flux, however, is how do you acquire knowledge? How do you hold down life long enough to know something about it? You cannot plot the path of a spiritual seed because it has no direct path. Life comprehended from this perspective is unpredictable—it will not continue in motion unless acted on by an outside force. As with any living organism, it will bounce all over the place. Occult philosophers were living in a world of biology animated by spirit, not a world of matter ruled by laws. To the occult philosopher, knowing something about nature involved connection, it required merging the eternal inner part of the self (the soul) with its counterpart in the object. This connection and the knowledge sought was really about the existential relationships inherent in the lived experience of things, all of which pointed to a transcendent other. The point was to know the living other. The epistemological values and the ontological orientation of sixteenth century occult philosophers were similar to those exhibited in the cave paintings of Altamira.

It was this quest that made alchemy attractive. Alchemy was less the science than the art of the sixteenth century occult philosopher. Fire was not simply for melting things down; it was for bringing things together. Fire was an elemental mantra to the invisible other, a vehicle invoked to embrace the world. The activity of alchemy was a noncognitive involvement. One was not trying to control a microcosmic world in the manner of a scientific experiment, one was trying to reinsert oneself in a macrocosmic event that included the self. The fire provoked a noncognitive, aconceptual medium for inserting oneself into things. Fire was the medium for the inner and outer to connect in a living relationship to the other.[25] Fire connected the soul of the alchemist with the soul of the object. The desired result was a knowledge of the life of things, a preverbal, preconceptual existential knowing. This was a knowing bred in the soul, not in the mind. The objective for the alchemist was to experience in "matter itself, at the very least an identity between the behavior of matter and the events in his own psyche."[26] This made possible the union of the eternal outer with the eternal inner. Alchemy was an art because it evolved in the indigenous relationship of the self to the other and not in a conscious construction of concepts. In a manner similar to how we try to understand our friends or family, alchemy sought to know the other from a

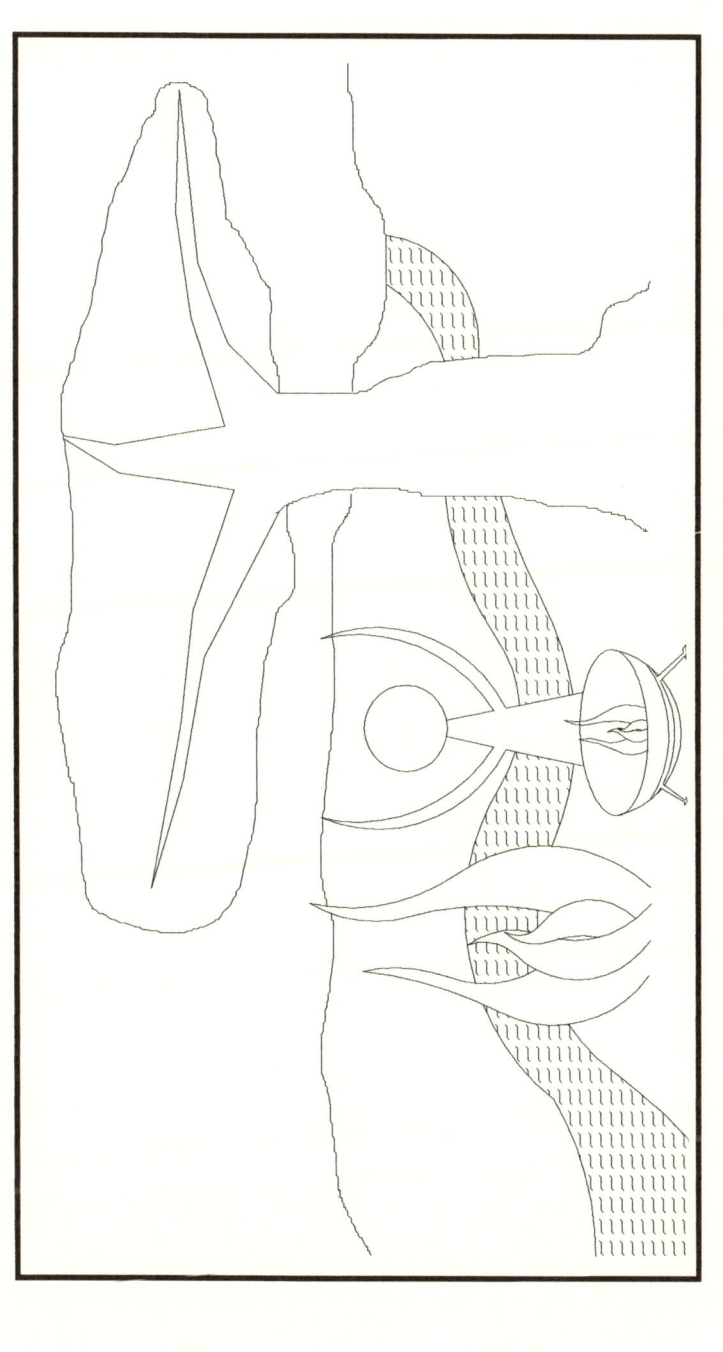

Figure 4.1: The Alchemical Process

58 *Mysticism and Experience*

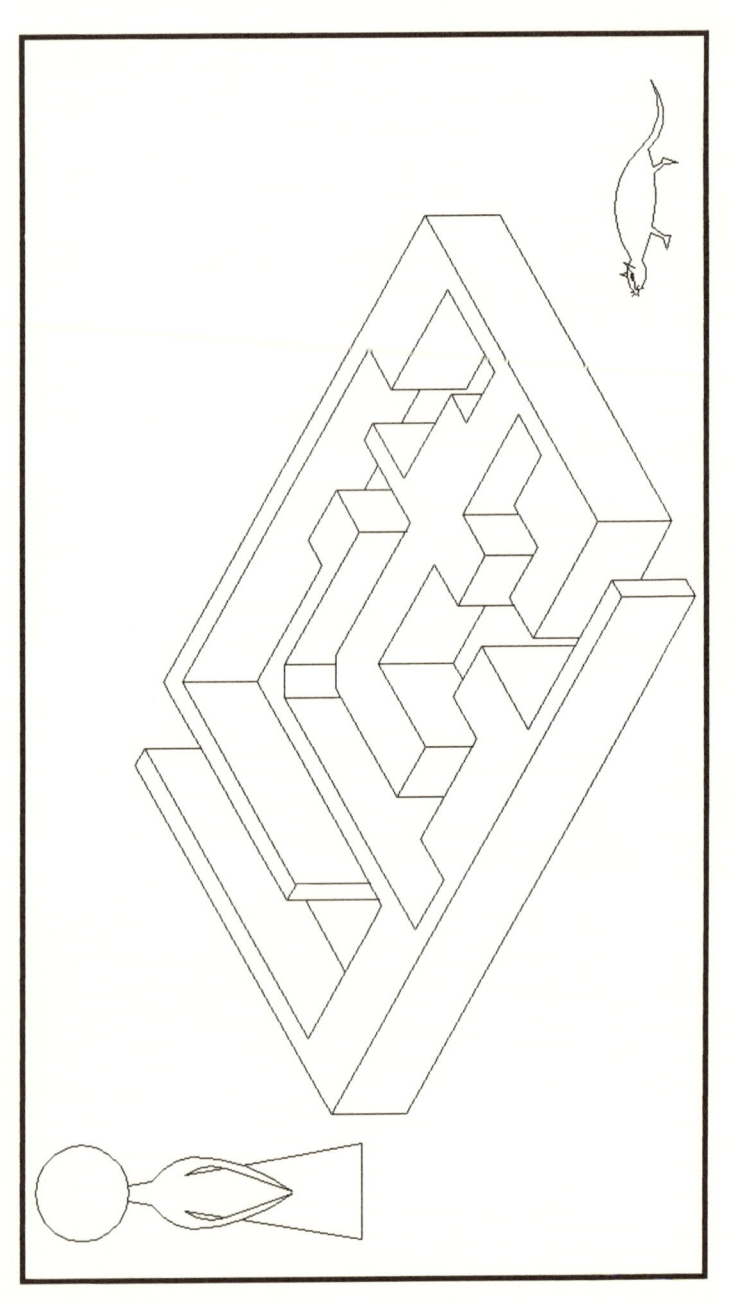

Figure 4.2: The Scientific Process

standpoint of love. Alchemy was art because it was a meditative, not a calculative activity. The point I am making is illustrated in Figure 4.1.

When Bacon defined the modern concept of experiment, he described a gulf that continues to this day between the knowledge acquired in the humanities or on a personal level and the hard sciences. The modern experiment proceeds from a presumed result (see Figure 4.2); it is designed to separate the knower from the known, and the ideal is to analyze without love.

Let me explore this a bit further. Carl Jung stressed that alchemy was a psychic activity, that when the alchemist was involved in melting down metals, he was projecting psychic experiences onto the events that occurred. The alchemical experiments, appearing as particular chemical processes, were really a projection of unconscious psychic activity. The experiences themselves, Jung said, had nothing to do with the matter itself; the alchemist was simply experiencing his own unconscious. According to Jung, the alchemist merely "recapitulated the history of man's knowledge of nature."[27] The alchemist was tapping into what Jung called the collective unconscious. At another point, however, Jung claims that the alchemist must experience "in matter itself, at the very least an identity between the behavior of matter and the events in his own psyche."[28] This seems more accurate to me. As an existential activity, alchemy was more than mental projections. There was a dynamic element included in the experiments. The activity was dialectical—the psychic event was activated by the alchemical activity, and if the individual remained true to the experiences, then an inner, spiritual, psychic seeing could take place. Alchemy and astrology were primal experiences arrived at when the conscious mind gave up control of the known. Engagement in alchemy opened up the possibility of being brought into a dimension of experience prior to rational consciousness. The activity of alchemy was a bridge that united the ontic one with the ontic other. Art (and mystical knowledge) may lie hidden in the human mind in its unconscious as Jung claimed, but its genesis into the conscious mind originates in experience.

It was this soul-based cosmology and Gnostic epistemology that created what appears to us the eccentric behavior and experiences of sixteenth century occult and alchemical philosophers. The Faustian legend, which helped establish the intellectual and ontological orientation of seventeenth century science, stressed reason heading to the stars, knowledge as power, knowing without feeling, and knowing without connection. This orientation was rejected by the true alchemist, who was engaged with life in a way difficult to fully imagine today. There was a stark immediacy to the experiences of sixteenth century occult philosophers, a directness of experience and feeling that enlivened and quickened the pulse of their investigations of nature. The occult philosophers of the sixteenth century—Paracelsus is only one of the more famous—lived as though they were (through their skin, membranes, nasal passages, saliva) coming in touch with reality in new way, a way not previously thought possible. Dirt under the fingernails, blood on the lips, smoke in the nose, the moon in the brain, the sun in the heart, and the great mystery of Eternal Nature there to be experienced and learned—not read about in the Bible and then known, not studied in the great tradition-bound texts of Aristotle, Galen, and their commentators but experienced.

Experience and feeling were the keys to knowledge for the occult alchemical philosophers of the sixteenth century; alchemists rejected the rational, tradition-bound science of the universities but did not adopt the Cartesian *cogito*. Rather, *experiencio ergo sum*. "We," I imagine them saying, "are feeling, experiencing, and knowing for the first time in centuries." Paracelsus was trying—as Hegel would later claim was the task of the modern world—to "free determinate thoughts from their fixity so as to give actuality to the universal, and impart to it a spiritual life."[29]

This enthusiasm for experiencing nature in order to understand it spurred science forward. It also made many of the centuries natural philosophers look scornfully on university professors and their claims to knowledge, a theme which, as I pointed out earlier, Galileo and other natural philosophers picked up with greater success but from a different angle in the seventeenth century. "We are alive," I hear Paracelsus exclaiming, "those university physicians and philosophers who live in books are dead." This was the refrain in Paracelsus's writings. Certainly, there is something literal about Paracelsus's famous statement to his university critics: "Let me tell you this," he yelled at a university committee, "every little hair on my neck knows more than you and all your scribes, and my shoe buckles are more learned than you Galen and Avicenna, and my beard has more experience than all your high colleges."[30] However, the statement is also nuanced with the inner sense of things we have been discussing in ways we have difficulty comprehending. Paracelsus was talking about the actual hairs on his neck, not the thoughts about the hairs on his neck that he had in his mind.

These were the intellectual paradigms that Böhme carried with him as he went on his inner journey. His unquestioned beliefs included a dualistic world of spirit/matter, a vision of life as activated spirit that had evolved from an original God, and a theory of knowledge that stressed the importance of illumination over rationalization, of meditation over calculation. Böhme knew and accepted the idea that life was a process of separation, and he believed his readers did also. There was no doubt or argument here. And because this was an assumed truth, there was much interest. Böhme's connection to his sociolinguistic history is obvious.

But inherent in this heritage was the means to get beyond it. Böhme's intellectual heritage set up conditions encouraging separation from his sociolinguistic past. His heritage de-emphasized the value of reason and rational constructions from previous perspectives. In stressing an autochthonic connection with nature, a connection that was really an opening up of the soul to acquire a union of souls, it required a meditative approach to the study of things. To gain a knowledge of nature, the sixteenth century occult philosopher had to enter into, via a meditative stand before things, an ontic relationship with things. He had to cease constructive rationalizing and a pragmatic orientation and allow the other to give something to him. The outer had to enter the inner, a relationship had to evolve based on

> Relinquishing of one's own familiar boundaries, a plunge into an unknown, fathomless realm of being. Through this it is possible to understand many things: active and the passive, hunter and hunted, eater and eaten, love and death—maybe about the soul and God.[31]

The point here is that in this particular ontological orientation to knowing something, one did not analyze the swamp, one opened oneself to it, jumped into it; one immersed oneself with the other and waited without thought for the experience and understanding to come. Revelation, moments of intuition that did not involve mental analysis, experiences that were not conditioned by intellectual filters, were the means to true understanding.

In a strong way, then, the sixteenth century alchemist, the occult philosopher, and the mystic turned the Western intellectual heritage around. From the Greeks to the scholastic philosophers to Böhme's scientific contemporaries (Descartes, Galileo, Bacon, Harvey, et al.), the higher mental levels of neurological activity have been lauded. Western philosophy has always looked at reason as superior to and transcending feeling and emotion and the latter as contaminating clear thinking and knowing.[32] But the point of a meditative orientation to reality was to get away from thought and back to a somatosensory connection with things, back to the ontic. In this condition one had the possibility of receiving a divine revelation.

Mystical knowledge has always been recognized by those who engage in it as a corrective to the purely rational. As anyone who has tried to meditate knows, stopping the chatter of the mind is not easy. But this was Böhme's achievement. He did what his heritage stressed was necessary to acquire knowledge. He had the revelations. This is what made him locally famous. Böhme was emptying his mind of thought and engaging ontically with things. Walking in fields, tasting apples, and making shoes were Böhme's fundamental experiences. His revelations were not so much an acting on a thing, but the act of the thing itself upon him. His intuitions were an opening himself up to things. His knowledge had something to do with what it was to eat an apple, something to do with the relationship of the apple to himself, and something to do with both the apple and his relationship with God.

These points are substantiated by Böhme's description of his revelations. They deal with the inner nature of things, with the sense of things acquired when one is merely open to the experiences of things and not analyzing them. Böhme claimed that he "saw and knew the essence of all essences, the ground and unground, the causes and primal conditions of this world."[33] When he explained his insights, he described them as the inner movement of eternal reality, its processes and changes, and the gradual manifestation of itself to its expression in the visible world. His project is therefore with the "entire and practical exactness of this motion of the eternal mystery of the spiritual world."[34] "My knowledge stands in this birth of the stars and in the midst where life is generated and breaks through death, and where the flowing spirit originates and shines through."[35] Böhme wanted to "recall life's beginning from which all originated."[36] He was the "new man [who] speculates into the midst of the Astral birth and sees the inner and outer wonders open."[37] The new man goes inside the already inner spiritual process to show how those processes proceed. The new man is Böhme, and he wanted to "show how the birth of all essences out of all mothers and origins, how one birth leads to another, and how the one is the cause of the other."[38]

CHAPTER 5

SPIRITUALISM AND THE INNER KNOWLEDGE OF GOD

> The question is nothing less than this: does the psychic in general—that is, the spirit or the unconscious—arise in us; or is the psyche, in the early stages of consciousness, actually outside us in the form of arbitrary powers with intentions of their own, and does it gradually come to take its place within us in the course of our psychic development?
>
> C. G. Jung

In order to make a point, let me exaggerate one. There are conversations that, in clarifying the parameters of an issue, cut a fissure through the thoughts and activities of future peoples, conversations that define a different perspective and create a different orientation. Martin Luther and the Holy Roman Emperor Charles V had one in 1521 and Christianity became two, then three, and so on. Wilhelm Leibniz and Samuel Clark (speaking for Newton) conversed during 1715-1716 and it effectively removed philosophical and moral issues from the quest for scientific knowledge. John Kennedy and Nikita Khrushchev had one in 1961 that established the mine and thine of East and West and prevented a third world war.

Also, we have a conversation that took place in 1525 between Schwenckfeld and Pomeranus of Wittenberg, a Lutheran minister (speaking for Luther). In clarifying the nature of spiritual knowledge and experience, that conversation effectively widened a gap that still exists. Schwenckfeld's and Pomeranus' conversation delineated the difference between inner and outer knowing, between a knowing that is absorbed and one that is made, between a knowing that affects the self and one that is there for use. Böhme was the epistemological heir to Schwenckfeld's arguments, and one of his primary objectives was to reaffirm the necessity of knowing the world in terms of its inner relationships and not simply in an objective outer manner.

Sixteenth Century Spiritualism

In 1525, Schwenckfeld wrote a letter and twelve questions to Martin Luther.[1] Those questions involved a dispute about the meaning of the Lord's Supper. The controversy that had begun earlier between Luther and Ulrich Zwingli involved the interpretation of the biblical passage that suggests the presence of Christ's body in the bread and his blood in the wine. Maintaining a literal reading of the Bible, Luther claimed that the bread was Christ's body, the wine his blood. Zwingli asserted that the bread only signified Christ's body.

Pondering the dilemma, Schwenckfeld realized still another problem: If the material merely signified Christ's body, how could it affect the soul, the spiritual nonmaterial part of the individual? On the other hand, if the bread were, as Luther claimed, Christ's body it would then be the case that even Judas and other sinners would be exonerated and saved merely by partaking of the Mass. Indeed, the entire physical universe might be thereby saved. To Schwenckfeld, both views were offensive. Judas and other sinners could not be saved for it seemed to Schwenckfeld that something more was required. Judas and others like him really could not have eaten of Christ's body, even though they swallowed the bread and wine in a ritual ceremony.

The conundrum could only be solved, Schwenckfeld believed, by realizing that the "body of Christ which is broken for us is an incorruptible food."[2] It was really a spiritual substance, not a material substance. As a spiritual substance it was impossible to be "received save by a spiritual true and living faith."[3] One had to be a true Christian believer to partake of Christ's body and blood. "Only the renewed believing souls . . . can partake of this delightful drink."[4] The "celestial bread, the incarnate word of God is [only] broken by the reborn internal man."[5]

Schwenckfeld's argument rested on a belief in a dualistic universe and a belief in the "fallenness" of humanity. His basic Neo-Platonic cosmology divided reality into a material substance and a spiritual essence. The former was in time and corruptible, the latter outside of time and eternal. To Schwenckfeld, the Holy Spirit was the center of the religious experience, and thus one's own inner spirit had to be engaged prior to partaking of and being affected by the body and blood of Christ. The point was not trivial. Schwenckfeld was asserting that an individual had to be spiritually enlightened in order to receive the spiritual benefits of the Mass. Those who were not, "receive from the Mass only the externals of the divine transaction, they cannot partake of the mysteries of the Holy Spirit."[6] An individual who expected to receive any benefit from the spiritual process of the Mass had to have some inner preparation or development prior to the event.

Three months after sending Luther the questions, Schwenckfeld went to talk with the reformer. The dialogue and subsequent conversations with Pomeranus of Wittenberg—Luther, being too busy or self-important (earlier shades of Clark speaking for Newton?), was unable to speak directly with Schwenckfeld—were beautifully recorded each night by Schwenckfeld. During these discussions, the epistemological and anthropological differences between Luther and Schwenckfeld became very clear.

Luther read the Bible literally. He also assumed that knowledge of the divine was possible through revealed scriptures. The Bible, Luther claimed, could be a direct source of knowledge (as could participation in the Mass). One could obtain knowledge of God and become spiritually enlightened through a close study of the Bible and by participating in Christian rituals and practices.

Schwenckfeld asserted the opposite belief. Yes, indeed, he argued, one could read the Bible with benefit; therefrom one could learn about the history and theology of the Christian religion. However, one could not comprehend the inner, deeper meaning of the Bible or Christianity unless one was spiritually enlightened. Schwenckfeld maintained that both the Bible and the Mass as external material things could not affect the spirit of the individual. By themselves, they "offer nothing to the inner essence of the soul."[7] No material object, no external statement, no outward actions could affect the inner man, the spirit. "We know," claimed Schwenckfeld, "that Christ instituted no external sign to strengthen faith and give assurance to conscience."[8] Inner truth had to come from the Spirit of God; the "signs add nothing to the inner essence of justification or the Holy Spirit's connection to man."[9] To Schwenckfeld, the sacraments and the Mass were not mediums for justification nor were they a source for the inner knowledge of God. The written or spoken word was not a source from which spiritual understanding could be acquired. Consequently, according to Schwenckfeld, for anyone who had not been spiritually enlightened, even the words of the Bible and the bread and wine of the Mass remained, at best, incomprehensible signs of a deeper reality, merely words or signs. As he told Pomeranus, "one must be justified previously and have partaken of the body of the Lord who would eat the bread of the Lord."[10]

The necessary priority Schwenckfeld was speaking about was a supernatural revelation, God directly enlightening the soul, a mystical experience. Schwenckfeld claimed that a deep personal understanding of Christ necessarily preceded full participation in the Christian message, and this understanding had to be given to the individual by the Holy Spirit. The individual could pray for understanding, faith, and salvation, could go to Church regularly and read the Bible daily, but individual volition was not necessarily going to produce a spiritually enlightening result. A transformation of self through divine intervention and grace was necessarily prior to spiritual comprehension. To Schwenckfeld, even faith was not something one worked at in the manner of Luther, but something given; faith was a freely given divine gift, not the reward of human effort. The pragmatic quest to achieve success in matters of the spirit was not assured of success. Something was given by God, something changed in oneself, and then understanding, faith, and salvation were acquired. Coincidentally, Schwenckfeld believed that he himself had received just such a revelation about the particular passage under discussion.

Unlike many German religious thinkers since Eckhart, Schwenckfeld did not postulate a synteristical element, a small piece of divine light (*Fünklein*) in the human soul, left there by God after the Fall.[11] He did assert the importance of an open, quiet (*Gelassenheit*), receptive heart as the first step in an individual's progress towards wisdom. Aside from this, there was little one could do to obtain Christian knowledge and understanding. One could not search for it, one could only be open to it. Wisdom was "not from human reason's work."[12] Understanding was to be had through the "working power of God and in the Holy Spirit."[13] Knowledge was something that came from and was given to the receptive individual.

Schwenckfeld's belief in the necessity of divine illumination for proper understanding rested, in part, on his interpretation of Adam's fall and Christ's rising. Prior to the Fall, humanity lived in spiritual union with God; human beings were spiritual, not material entities. This union ended after the Fall, and it was not until Christ that humanity was given a second chance at becoming spiritual and again entering into the internal, eternal world of God. To do this, one had to shed the earthly, fleshly, outer life. One had to give up the "Old

Adam" and "put on the new man . . . who is created after God, and righteousness, holiness, and divine truth."[14] This refrain runs from Schwenckfeld through Weigel and Böhme. It can be translated not only as a salvific injunction but also as part of an epistemological/anthropological doctrine, a particular approach to living and being in the world.

Epistemologically, Schwenckfeld was asserting the priority and exclusivity of the Holy Spirit in the form of a revelation given to man as a source of knowledge. This altered the inner psychological state of the individual, presenting him with a new realization, a fresh orientation or understanding about the Bible, the universe, and God. In the realm of Christian knowledge, this reorientation was more important than historically developed and advanced knowledge—such was human commentary, revelation was divine statement. And truth came before symbol, concept, or metaphor. Words and reason do not make better Christians. They will produce at most, he claimed, a "short lived carnal emotion of simulated faith."[15] The Protestant principle that an individual contributes nothing to his own salvation was now extended to the realm of personal Christian knowledge.

Anthropologically, this subjective intuitive knowledge demanded a particular lifestyle, described as giving up the Old Adam, putting on the new man, or "following Christ." This, of course, was a historically developed concept; it had a history. But it was also a statement on a mode of being that aimed at allowing the self to escape from history and from the world of idea, words, and language. Putting on the new man was a prescription for how to avoid the pitfalls of reason, rational knowledge, and absorption in the present so that an inner, eternal knowledge derived from the Holy Spirit could be acquired. The point was to forget one's history, to allow oneself to transcend it. Consequently, the relationship one had with the world was not the active, seeking rationale of the academy, nor was it the pragmatic orientation of the businessman. Following Christ was a way of attaining release from the historically conditioned interpretation of things.[16] The task was not to analyze but to receive. Understanding the inner word of the Bible required a hearing "without recourse to human interests."[17] This was "not a metaphysical doctrine but a subjective mental state wherein trust lay in God and not in man."[18] As such, the epistemological and anthropological principles assumed here were really analogical descriptions of the particular mode of being most likely to result in reception of divine knowledge. The goal was to create a mode of being that would bring one into closer relationship with the eternal spheres of reality.

Schwenckfeld never outlined exactly what this ahistorical existential stand before the world and God should be. That would be done by Böhme. Nor would he fully articulate his theories and break from Luther until 1526. But, as he struggled through these issues, he helped redefine the Reformation along radical spiritual, epistemological, and anthropological lines. The ideas he had articulated became part of an outsider arm of German Lutheranism. To be Schwenckfeldian was to be anti-institutional, to be Schwenckfeldian was to be a *Schwärmer* (Enthusiast), a spiritualist. This inward religion of the spirit gained strength throughout the sixteenth century and led Sebastian Franck, fellow reformer, to comment:

> There already are in our times three distinct faiths which have a large following, the Lutheran, Zwinglian and Anabaptist; and a fourth is well on the way to birth, which will dispense with external preaching, ceremonies, sacraments, and offices as unnecessary, and which seeks solely to gather among all peoples an invisible, spiritual Church in the unity of the spirit and of a faith to be governed wholly by the eternal, invisible world of God, without external means, as the apostolic Church was governed before its apostasy, which occurred after the deaths of the apostles.[19]

Although Franck claimed to have been disposed toward Plato, Plotinus, and Hermes Trismagistus, Franck, too, was a product of the German mystical tradition and the Lutheran reform movement. His philosophical concerns were with the spiritual understanding of the inner meaning of the divine being, and like Schwenckfeld, he maintained that people can only find the true meaning of Christ in the depths of their hearts, not in books, not even the Bible, for "the Scriptures must give witness to the spirit, never against it."[20] Knowledge had to move from the Holy Spirit downward as a form of illumination. But, although Franck's recognition and support of the new "invisible, spiritual Church" was important for its growth, Weigel was the important conduit of this religious message to the seventeenth century, and especially to Böhme.

Weigel, a Lutheran minister born a couple of generations after Schwenckfeld and Franck, remained within the Church throughout his life, but he was not an espouser of Lutheran orthodox doctrine. Intellectually maturing in the second half of the sixteenth century, Weigel participated in the revival of Paracelsian philosophy and personally experienced the constriction of religious expression following the entrenchment of Lutheran orthodoxy in the last quarter of the century. Like Schwenckfeld and Franck, Weigel's thoughts on knowledge and understanding began with a Neo-Platonic cosmology that separated the physical and spiritual planes of existence. He accepted a dualism between spirit and matter and thus his entire anthropological position was based on a series of juxtapositions. For example, the following contrary life choices were offered to his readers:

Adam	Christ
Disbelief	Belief
Flesh	Spirit
Nature	Grace
Old man	New man
Darkness	Light
Tree of Evil	Tree of Light
Death	Life[21]

The list was loaded, of course, and Weigel encouraged the individual to choose the style of life congruent with the ideas expressed in the right column. To do so meant one was directed by one's inner spirit—this was the true essence of man. It was so because God himself was pure sprit and the universe originated out of spirit (Weigel sometimes used the Paracelsian elements mercury, salt, and sulfur to describe the spiritual aspects of reality).[22] To Weigel, therefore, inner life was essential life.[23] The actively engaged spiritually maturing individual was so to the extent that he was shedding the earthly life and going towards the inner life of the soul. Additionally, in the tradition of Eckhart, but unlike Schwenckfeld, Weigel claimed that existence of a synteristical element in the human soul: "He is in us in the inward ground of the soul . . . in the spirit stands the realm of God, not in the body."[24] To be actively engaged in Christian life demanded shedding one's earthly life. "The perfect God in the inward ground of the soul would be found, felt, and tasted as soon as the creature ceased, then God would step in."[25] He claimed that the individual had to die to himself. "The Adam in us must die and Christ must climb up and live."[26] More Schwenckfeldianisms.

Given this cosmology and spiritually founded conception of man, Weigel's epistemology stressed the relationship between the spirit of God and the soul of the individual. He claimed the necessary priority of divine intervention or illumination for knowledge: "Christ comes to us through grace," he maintained.[27] Thus, as Steven Ozment noted, the "soul's first interaction was with the exemplary world of the divine mind, [its] original orientation and alliance is vertical, not horizontal."[28] To Weigel, "all our sciences, arts, studies, actions, offices, vocations, industries, labors, and kinds of life . . . ought to be drawn forth on earth from the light of nature . . . all comes from the will of God."[29] Weigel denied the power of the letter and other externals to affect the inner person; as with Schwenckfeld, the scriptures were barren to the unenlightened soul. Spirit preceded letter. Enlightenment preceded being, completed being was knowing. Even knowledge of nature was to come through the "light of nature." "This world to the outer eyes is too gross and incomprehensible, but to the inner eye it is small and comprehensible. Whoever wants to study and measure things with the outer sensual eyes and learn things with the five senses, he does not belong in my wisdom of Christ and remains totally stupid."[30] This would seem to put an end to objective studies of nature and empirical analyses of the world. But the issue was not "Do not study nature." The issue was "Do not base your studies of nature first of all on the five senses." A difficult task indeed, but one that Böhme was going to claim he accomplished.[31]

Weigel's importance lies as much in asserting Schwenckfeldian epistemology as in beginning to adopt it toward the study of nature while simultaneously maintaining the necessity of a passive receptive position before the world. Weigel had been influenced by Paracelsus and the growing interest in the study of nature (to Paracelsus and Weigel, nature was the second book of God), but he remained true to Schwenckfeldian epistemology and anthropology.

The last quarter of the sixteenth century and the first quarter of the seventeenth century saw the solidification of orthodox Lutheranism. The Formula of Concord in 1577 gave Lutherans a closed system of theological doctrine and set forth the institutional interpretation of the Bible. As a counterforce to Lutheran orthodoxy, the writings of radical Lutherans such as Franck and Schwenckfeld (as well as radical natural philosophers with similar knowledge claims such as Paracelsus et al.) became popular. Small clandestine study groups, often organized and moderated by the local minister, proliferated. When the local minister took a conservative theological stand, clandestine study groups evolved. Questions about cosmology, natural philosophy, and Christology were being discussed throughout the cities and small towns of Germany by noblemen and commoners alike. And, despite the solidification of the orthodox position, many Lutherans continued to proclaim the importance of "inward spirituality."

Johann Andreä (a Lutheran minister, the son of a Lutheran minister, and the person most frequently associated with the Rosicrucians) elaborated similar epistemological and anthropological ideas in his Chemical Wedding (1616). The Rosicrucian tracts themselves (1614-1616) echo the ideas we have been discussing—either in ridicule or seriously, but in either case with some importance. The publication of these tracts aroused a heated battle of pamphlets, essays, and even books, some requesting information about the supposedly secret society with secret knowledge, others questioning the validity of the knowledge claims. Robert Fludd, physician to James I of England, bemoaned his lack of intuitive knowledge and defended the Rosicrucians in print in a futile attempt at being contacted by them. Andrea Libavius expostulated that their reform must indeed be very private because he could not discover it. Nor, he continued, did it have anything to do with the sciences or arts or anything else that might be reformed by man. Johann Arndt's *Vier Bücher vom Wahren Christentum* stressed a similar spiritualist message (and laid the foundation for the Pietist movement). This was an enthusiast's period and the questions about inner, intuitive knowledge and the path to that knowledge were significant concerns.[32]

Yet, it was Böhme who extended the inner message the farthest. Böhme claimed to have received all his ideas from the Holy Spirit and offered, in a large corpus, an entire cosmology based on his revelations. Böhme had been raised as a Lutheran and was faithful throughout his life. His ideas on a knowledge of inner truths were stimulated in a study group in Görlitz, Germany, his birthplace. The group was organized by Möller when Böhme was in his middle twenties. Called the "Conventicle of God's Real Servants," it was a group in the "true mystical tradition."[33] The purpose of the group was to study Möller's many books, poems, and essays on the German mystics of the past and to discuss the eternal spirit of Christianity. Möller was not dedicated to the orthodox interpretation of Christianity.[34] He professed being a Christian spiritualist who stressed the "heart over the letter, Christianity over doctrinairism."[35] While part of this study group, Böhme met many of Görlitz's noble class, most of whom claimed to be followers of Schwenckfeld. One of them, Michael Ender, became Böhme's best friend and was instrumental in circulating Böhme's first book.[36]

Böhme called Schwenckfeld and Weigel his two "great masters,"[37] and aside from Paracelsus, these are the only two authors he begrudgingly professed learning anything from (he could not have claimed otherwise if all his knowledge was intuitively derived). In his brief comments on them (eleven paragraphs in his entire corpus), he acknowledges their "great value" but contends that they "did not quite comprehend enough."[38] Schwenckfeld was not clear on Christ's true being and he had never fully understood the (Protestant) principle.[39] Weigel had the same problem. For clarification of these points, Böhme directed the reader of the letter to his own books. Then, drawing a connection between them and himself, he claimed that "nevertheless, they did enough considering the age [in which they live]."[40] It was now left to Böhme to extend their ideas.

And extend them he did. Except for a four year hiatus, when Böhme was forced to put down his pen after his first book angered the new pastor, he wrote tome after tome, more than twenty books and pamphlets in half as many years. All his books, he claimed, were not a result of his own efforts but the consequence of a series of divine revelations he had had. All his knowledge was a received inner knowledge.

> I cannot say that [my knowledge] is my understanding or reason's work, but I know it for a wonder in which God revealed great things... because I am not learned nor do I have art or wisdom, therefore I must write from another school. I am a poor and simple implement.[41]

But whereas Schwenckfeld claimed insight into certain passages in the Bible, Böhme asserted complete inner and, ultimately, outer worldly understanding.[42] Böhme went even further and denied the importance of experience because it related to things that one had grown accustomed to in the education process; something besides reason and historically determined experience, he exclaimed, had brought understanding to him.

As with Schwenckfeld, Böhme believed a specific existential stand before the world was necessary in order to receive divine knowledge. He described the anthropology behind the understanding in the same terms as Schwenckfeld. One put on the new man, one followed Christ, not Adam. To Böhme, following Christ was a "now-seeing," a "sinking down," a "nongrasping"—something that did not come "through self-will." Böhme claimed that the moments when he escaped historically determined experience, had an intuition, and acquired a different knowledge of the world, he was now-seeing—an immediate, nonmediated connection to reality. One absented oneself from rational structures and was silent before the world. Then, through the power of imagination, the individual might sink down deep into the self, into a deeper source of things, into the "eternal will and abyss." It was here that an individual came in contact with the eternal element behind all things because the self (and the mind) had its origins in the center of nature. It was at the point when one entered into the archetypal element of the self and touched the "mother's womb" (the archetypal element in the universe) that one could receive an intuitive and fresh understanding of things. Böhme claimed that he had experienced just such a regression and the consequent absorption of eternal knowledge. Böhme had mastered the Enthusiasts' epistemological/anthropological prescription of detachment from the Old Adam in himself, achieved a different stand before things ("un-Adamic"), and consequently, he had an immediate spiritual connection with the eternal spirit or realm of the universe. He described such events:

> The harmony of hearing, seeing, feeling, tasting, and smelling is the true intellectual life. When one power enters into another they embrace one another in the sound, and when they penetrate each other they mutually awaken and know each other and in this knowledge consists the true understanding ... eternal wisdom of the One which is all.[43]

The existential condition Böhme described here implies an openness to the world with one's entire being. Seeing involved creating a living harmony with the other. The important actions are to embrace, to mutually awaken, to enter into another. An embrace, the conceptual ideal, was the result of a noncalculating mind. As Böhme embraced the other and the other embraced him, soul to soul. In this embrace, both beings were mutually awakened. This mutual awakening and knowing of each other was "true understanding . . . eternal wisdom." Embrace another being in its entirety, touch its inner content, and you are engaging in the eternal. By harmonizing with another, Böhme was bringing together the diversity of experience and comprehending the One from which all things originated.

A Modern Man

By 1612, Böhme had become quite famous in his home town, Görlitz, but this was a mixed blessing. Connected with Schwenckfeld, he was recognized by conservative Lutherans as an Enthusiast. He was then harassed, forced by the new pastor, Gregor Richter, to stop writing, and finally, to leave Görlitz. Orthodox power was correct in these judgments. Böhme clearly believed his views were Christologically superior and closer to the real message of Christ than those expressed by the local pastor; after all, Böhme got his understanding from a Divine source. Böhme was the mystic in the parish, an inkblot on the manuscript of doctrinal knowledge. His intuitive understanding of God and the universe did not correspond with doctrinal message. But something had changed and Böhme was clearly talking less about the salvific powers of the Eucharist than about cosmology.

Böhme's generation was that of the fathers of the Scientific Revolution: Galileo, Harvey, Kepler, and Bacon were his contemporaries. The Copernican thesis had thrown the universe out of joint. Paracelsian nature philosophy was turning more heads than Lutheran doctrinal issues. Affected by these historical changes, Böhme's interests (but not his epistemology and anthropology) changed. The questions he asked were different. Schwenckfeld and Weigel focused on the Bible and salvation. Böhme focused on nature, the cosmos, and the individual's relationship to both. Schwenckfeld, Weigel, Franck, and Böhme claimed revelation as the source of knowledge, but because they had different interests, their revelations were different. Böhme's interest in nature and his disillusionment following his awareness of the destruction of the cosmos by Copernicus precipitated a revelation that illuminated how the cosmos evolved. Böhme had to answer questions about God's role in the cosmos, not questions about the effective power of the Eucharist.

Although Böhme's epistemology and the anthropology have essential consistency with his predecessors, a radical shift had taken place: The issues at stake were no longer how to attain salvation in a comprehensible cosmos but how to comprehend an incomprehensible cosmos and man's and God's place in this cosmos. Böhme wrote books about the origin of the cosmos. His books describe the process of creation from God's first self-conscious stirring prior to creation to the actual creation of the physical matter of the universe. His intuitions were about the prephysical (noncorporeal) structures of the universe and how they evolved to form the physical universe.

Böhme saw himself as part of the growth of the new sciences, which he recognized as a positive intellectual event. He accurately perceived the mathematical and observational aspects of these sciences and claimed that his and their work were "one body, one tree, bearing one and the same fruit."[44] Nevertheless, he distinguished the new mathematically governed sciences from his own intuitive science. And although he admitted, "I have not yet studied all their arts, nor do I know how to measure circles and use their mathematical instruments and compasses," he admonished that they, too, had much to learn.[45] The new scientists, he claimed, continuing a battle begun a hundred years earlier in a different sociocultural context, were only looking at the external visible world. They were investigating only the letter of nature.

> The highly experienced masters of astrology or the starry arts...know the course and effects of the stars...and [they] have a true foundation which I know to be so, but their knowledge stands only in the house of death in the outward comprehensibility.[46]

Böhme was quick to point out that their empirical observations offered only one part of the picture. They "behold with the eyes of the body," and therefore the "root...has remained hidden to them."[47] It was up to Böhme with his intuitive knowledge of the eternal spiritual realm of reality to complete the picture drawn by the new scientists.

> I will not build upon their ground, but as a laborious careful servant, I will dig away the earth from the root, that thereby men may see the whole tree with its root stock, branches, twigs, and fruits.[48]

He would establish his own system and explanation of things and it would complement their externally derived, humanly constructed science because his centered around the interior meaning and processes of nature and because his knowledge was a consequence of the influence of the Holy Spirit.

Perhaps Böhme's interpretation of the empirical and observational aspects of the scientific revolution were not totally accurate. As with Schwenckfeld, Franck, and Weigel, Böhme's epistemological concerns were for a universal truth that transcended time. Böhme's anthropological stand was designed to work through issues that take place in time so that a knowledge could be received that was beyond time. If we look at Böhme's scientific contemporaries, especially Kepler and Galileo and later Descartes, there is some way in which this too was their concern. They wanted to escape the corruption of the senses with a more certain truth—a truth of the mind. Galileo was convinced that knowledge of nature preceded investigation of nature. I am thinking especially of the passage in the *Dialogue on the Two Chief World Systems* where the Copernican theorist taunts the Aristotelian empiricist about his inability to recognize the real truth about motion.[49] He then proceeds to describe the thought experiment of perfectly round balls and perfectly smooth incline planes. Galileo did not need physical experiments to recognize certain truths about how nature works. He recognized such things in his mind, and he could get others to do it too. Just think about it, he said.

But Böhme was right, and the distinction he draws defines what distinguishes an inner, intuitive (mystical) knowledge from scientific knowledge. On a broader scale, Böhme's position describes exactly how much the scientific revolution was a watershed in the intellectual and ontological values of the modern world. Galileo's statement and the epistemological and anthropological stand it supports mark the ascension to dominance of the scientific method; it marks a difference between an inner and outer knowledge, between a knowledge born from rational reflection and one derived from a receptive noncognitive stand before things. Böhme's knowledge comes from an embrace, Galileo's from an assessment. Böhme's knowledge comes when he quiets his rational mind and absorbs or is given the living pulse of things. Galileo rationally abstracts from a theoretically developed, historically derived orientation to things to understand the ideal patterns of things. He fits the world and God into the theories. The one is a knowledge above the lived experience of things, the other within. Both modes of understanding have their place. Unfortunately, I believe that deference to Galileo's mode has subsumed modern consciousness.

CHAPTER 6

MADNESS AND KNOWLEDGE

> What did we do when we unchained this earth from its sun? Whither is it moving now? Whither are we moving now? Away from all suns? Are we not plunging continually? Backward, sideward, forward, in all directions? Is there any up or down left? Are we not straying as through an infinite nothing? Do we not feel the breath of empty space? Has it not become colder? Is not night and more night coming on all the while?
>
> Friedrich Nietzsche

There is an interesting parable in Nietzsche's The Gay Science entitled "The Madman." A madman, entering a small lazy town, begins screaming "I seek God! I seek God!" The townspeople converge around the man and start mocking him. "Did he get lost?" said one. "Did he lose his way like a child?" said another. "Or is he hiding? Is he afraid of us?" The litany of abuse continues until the madman speaks up. I shall tell you where he has gone, he says, "we have killed him." The madman then voices a series of questions to the incredulous people, starting with the above and continuing with "Do we not smell anything yet of God's decomposition? . . . How shall we, the murderers of all murderers, comfort ourselves? . . . What water is there for us to clean ourselves?" Finally, in the face of derisive laughter of the townspeople, the madman throws the lantern he had brought down on the pavement and hustles out of the town. "I come too early. My time has not yet come. This deed is still more distant from them than the most distant stars—and yet they have done it themselves."

Nietzsche is making a number of points that are relevant here. The first, and by no means the most important, is that not only the madman but the normal townspeople know that God is dead. This is hardly news; to the townspeople it is boring. Hence the mockery of the mad by the sane. What makes the madman mad and distinguishes him from the sane, and this is another point, is that the madman recognizes that consequences result from this, the most momentous event in history, and the townspeople do not. Hence Nietzsche's mockery of the sane, and laudation of the mad. The madman carries the lantern—the light that reveals the truth—because he has looked at, accepted, and understood the consequences the truths of science have had on our understanding of and belief in God. The madman is so because of his intellectual honesty; the sane are so because of their willingness to lie to themselves.

Nietzsche's general philosophic goal of destroying sacred cows and asking twentieth century individuals to face their own deceits began with the destruction of the venerable tradition of ancient values. Most of those values had sprung from the Judeo-Christian tradition. Writing during the last quarter of the nineteenth century, Nietzsche accepted that the truths of science did away with God and asked subsequent generations to create new values, because the old ones no longer had a foundation. Nietzsche was sane (intellectually honest) and therefore a madman. For Nietzsche, there was no other alternative: The pervasive rationality of science, its principles, and its truths were secure. No doors were open for a divine being.

At the end of the sixteenth century, Böhme was sane (by Nietzsche's definition)—therefore he was a madman. Three centuries before Nietzsche, Böhme recognized that scientific truths destablized ancient perceptions and threw the world out of joint. Historical developments in human thought once again played a role in the mystic's life. Böhme, like Nietzsche, was destablized by the growth of science: The new theories attacked the ethos Böhme had assumed valid. He began to ponder the problems the new sciences created for his religious beliefs. Böhme's antidote to the growth of scientific truth, however, was not Nietzsche's. His ruminations led to his mystical intuitions; the intuitions provided him with an answer to the new sciences. Let me explain.

I have already made clear that Böhme was a historical man; the parameters of his thought were conditioned by the historical dialogues he heard growing up in Görlitz in the latter half of the sixteenth century. Under the rubric of sixteenth century occult philosophy, Böhme acquired a mishmash of Paracelsian, Gnostic, alchemical, and magical assumptions about nature, knowledge, man, and God. From Schwenckfeld and other radical Lutheran spiritualists he acquired spiritualist views that he never abandoned; he remained a Lutheran throughout his life, even after being forced to leave Görlitz by the Lutheran pastor. However, a fundamental characteristic of the occult and spiritualist dialogues that Böhme absorbed consisted of an epistemology and a derivative ontology that necessitated breaking from the dialogue if a personal, inner knowledge of reality was to be had. The diachronic content of Böhme's personal history provided for the possibility of breaking from that history and having a nonlinguistically mediated experience. Indeed, this inner, intuitive, received, knowledge was recognized by Böhme as fundamental for any real understanding. Böhme inherited from his occult, Paracelsian, and radical Lutheran spiritualist predecessors the belief that an intuitive, inner understanding of things was, if not superior to a rational assessment and development of things, at least equal to it.

Granted that mystical insight is never something taken but something given and received and that anyone at any time could be given a mystical experience, it is nevertheless true that openness to understanding is preparation for it. Böhme wanted to understand and this wanting, in conjunction with his epistemological and ontological heritage, helped give him the possibility of receiving understanding. One must itch before the need to scratch occurs. In terms of the desire for understanding, Böhme's itch was cosmological and theological doubts that arose from his recognition and understanding of the consequences of the theories of the new sciences. The synchronic factors that undermined Böhme's trust in things and led him to begin ruminating in the manner suggested by his heritage revolved around the growth of science.

Let me add that despite his intellectual heritage and despite his desire to understand, there is no reason to suppose that Böhme should have had those mystical experiences. Much less should we think that he should have had a series of illuminations spanning twelve years and from this fountain withdraw enough understanding to write the books he did. Mystical experience is not conditional but transcendental. Up to the point of the experience itself, however, Böhme was scratching a huge itch, an itch given to him by various new ideas about cosmology and knowledge he had heard about.

God as Process

The constant of course is change. Every era is unsettling for those involved. The turn from the sixteenth to the seventeenth century, however—I use this as a symbolic turning point—was as significant, on an intra-European, even a world historical level, as perhaps any centurial shift since the first century C.E. By 1600, the earth's place in the universe had been shattered by the Copernican thesis, Europe's place as the center of the earth had been shattered by Columbus, Rome's place as the center of religion had been shattered by Luther; and the scholastic hold on knowledge had been undermined by the humanist retrieval of ancient texts.

It is difficult to imagine the consequences of these events. When armies march through towns or storms destroy houses, when illness or other natural or human calamities occur, lives are shattered. Humans are made uneasy after such events. Their sense of physical security is shaken. But while physical disasters have their consequences, they are comprehensible insofar as they are the result of a series of cause and effect relationships. Copernicus and Luther, however, were assaults not on the body's sense of security but on the psyche's; their theories attacked the ethos that had governed perceptions and lent order to the world for some 1500 years. Copernicus unchained the earth from the sun, as Nietzsche was claiming, and destroyed the canopy of certainty that had existed for 1500 years. Luther bifurcated the idea of Christianity, throwing into doubt 1500 years of belief in one Church. The seemingly unassailable assumptions about which people gave hardly a thought, and yet on which they based their most important theories about God, nature, values, and morals, were thrown open for view and criticism because they no longer had a foundation.

Not everyone, of course, realizes the implications and feels the psychological effect of ethotic change. Nietzsche's parable still holds true. It is only the honest who are mad, those ostracized by virtue of their understanding, those who comprehend the consequences of loosing values from their moorings. The rest of us drift in empty space without conscious awareness or cling tenaciously to one or another prejudice. This drifting, whether conscious or not, creates the psychological tenor of the modern world. No moorings. "All that is solid melts into air," as Marx put it.

Copernicus, one could argue, inadvertently started the demooring by loosening the chains that tied the earth to the sun. Published in 1543, *The Revolution of the Heavenly Spheres* began to undermine the cosmology that had underwritten the theology, that had underwritten morality and given credence to the values of the Western world for a couple of millennia. By 1600, when Böhme was reaching intellectual maturity, the Copernican thesis was no longer an esoteric work from an obscure Polish mathematician and astronomer. If the population of Görlitz was typical of cities in Europe at that time, some members of the place were talking about the theory. Böhme was one of them.

It is difficult to establish exactly Böhme's intellectual position in relationship to his contemporaries or even whether he had read specific authors. He was aware of many of the scientific ideas of his day, especially the new cosmological theories, the emphasis on mathematics and rationality in scientific work, and, as pointed out in the previous chapter, the stress on empirical observation as the basis of objective knowledge. He mentioned the use of instruments to investigate nature and that some of the new descriptions of reality involved the use of new rules and formulas.

The application of mathematics to the study of nature was acknowledged by Böhme: "Some of the astrologers," he noted, "have undertaken to measure how far [the sun's] orb and the circumference of its supposed motion."[1] His comprehension of the Copernican theory was basic but accurate. The "sun has its own royal place to itself and does not go away from that place where it came to be.... The earth moves itself about and runs with the other planets as in a wheel, round the sun. The earth does not remain staying in one place, but runs around in a year."[2] He adds that the "planets are peculiar bodies of their own which have a corporeal property of themselves and are not bound to any settled or fixed place, but only to their circles, orbs, or spheres."[3]

Böhme acknowledged as valid the new theories that replaced the vaulted, enclosed, geocentric universe with a heliocentric and (by 1600) infinite universe.[4]

> People have always maintained that heaven was several thousand miles from the earth, and that God lived there. [But] recently several physicists have brought forth very strange things. Before this...I believed that was how the heavens were, enclosed within a round circle... high over the stars.[5]

The apparent validity of the theories disturbed him. The grain of sand in Böhme's mind was that "the highly experienced masters of astrology or the starry arts...know the course of the stars...and they have a true foundation that I know in spirit to be so."[6] The self-contained unity of Ptolemaic cosmology wherein everything had its place and the relationship of each to each were known dissolved before his eyes like an apparition. His sense of order was shattered. Where was God now? What threads bring us together? He moaned that whenever anyone views

> [The] deep above the earth one sees nothing but stars and clouds of water and then one thinks surely there must be

> some other place where the deity lives . . . then one thinks
> God made this out of nothing, but how then could God be
> in this being or how could a being be God himself.[7]

The reality of an infinite universe, an openness without end, with no secure place for God (or himself) unsettled him. In his own words, he fell into a "deep melancholy and sadness whenever [he] viewed the great deep of this world."[8]

The emptiness Böhme's understanding of an infinite universe gave him was exacerbated because the positive aspects of life no longer had warrant and the negative retribution was no longer certain. The good had no claim to a heavenly salvation, the bad might not go to hell. Now that the position of God in the universe was in question, the foundation for hope, morality, and values was also questionable. How do you explain the evil and horror of life? Was everything, as Nietzsche would later proclaim, justified? Was absolutely nothing required and everything valid? Doubts about the nature of evil in the post-Copernican world are more problematic than the trials of Job. God's silence might not be intentional but consequential—there is nothing there of consequence. The negative was just that. Böhme experienced this. He looked around and noticed "in all things good and evil, love and hate . . . in the elements as well as the creatures, and that in the world things went as well with the pious as impious."[9] The fabric of values and morals was pilling, even unraveling.

Böhme's angst was modern, and Böhme was certainly one of the first modern, even post-modern men. It was not simply that Böhme understood that the Copernican theory was true, that he believed that the sun was the center of the universe, and that the universe was much larger than the enclosed vaulted universe of the Middle Ages, that made him modern. The sane townspeople are not modern because they lack awareness that their lives are without anchor. Belief in science and its truths about nature does not in itself define the essence of the modern world. Böhme understood the cause of the despair of the modern world as well as Nietzsche: If the scientific facts about the world are true and if the world works as science supposes, then where is the place for God, for spirit, for the transcendent? And if there is no place for these things, what basis do we have for our values? How do you establish values, how can you justify them?

Böhme's historically generated experience in 1600 (prior to his intuitions) was emptiness, alienation, and melancholy. By 1600, a townsman had become mad—Böhme had lost a "sense of ultimate coherence or meaning in the cosmic environment."[10] This was a historically conditioned experience. He was no longer content. What to do?

Several adaptations or solutions exist. Nietzsche took one of them: He accepted the picture of nature science had described and the impossibility of God's existence the scientific theories implied. Recognizing the implications of science led him to jettison all values based on God and to proclaim that the new philosophical imperative of the modern world was to establish a new set of values based on the vision of nature and life science described. Nietzsche threw God out with the Ptolemaic cosmology and the Aristotelian epistemology. We now live in a Godless world. Such was Nietzsche's belief. How shall we live in this world, and what shall our new values be? Such were Nietzsche's questions.

Another approach is to ignore scientific truths altogether and proceed in one's religious and daily life as though nothing ever happened, as though Galileo, Newton, and Einstein and what they postulated and discovered never existed. Adopt a stoic ignorance. Mock the issues, refuse to consider them. This was the tack the townspeople in Nietzsche's parable took. A third alternative is to simply deny the truths of science on a theological ground. The Catholic and Protestant Churches adopted this position; Galileo's observations and telescope did not prove anything. His pronouncements were wrong. As we know, Galileo recanted his theories in 1636 and the Church their condemnation of Galileo's theories in 1994.

A modern alternative (becoming increasingly popular, interestingly enough, among many scientists) is to try to fit God, theology, and morals into the theoretical framework of science.[11] Put God within the glove, so to speak, of science. In this attempt to rescue God, the individual approaches God by assuming that the truths of science are absolute and unequivocal but then asks, how can we think about God and the values and hopes the belief in God spawned given our understanding of how nature works? Here, as explained by science, are the parameters of the really real, how can we now fit God into this picture?

Another possibility exists, one Böhme became aware of after he received his mystical intuitions about God and cosmology. Böhme acknowledged the validity of the scientific method and accepted the truths about nature it provided. With this he had no problem. But he also recognized that scientific truths were a result of a particular rational and pragmatic orientation to things and that this orientation was not some apotheosis of orientations that disallowed all prior attempts by human beings to comprehend the world. Nor did it permit a complete experience of things. Then as now, the belief that the scientific perspective has made all other means to knowledge obsolete, smacks of a hubris similar to medieval Christianity.

Böhme did not accept this assertion. To him, the scientific orientation did not provide the final and only means to understand reality. "Their knowledge stands . . . in outward comprehensibility." "They behold with the eyes of the body," and therefore the "root . . . has remained hidden to them."[12] According to Böhme, they were investigating only the letter, the concept of nature, and consequently, they understood only that sphere. Böhme would "dig away the earth from the root, that thereby men may see the whole tree with its root stock, branches, twigs, and fruits."[13]

This was not a trite insight. At some level, Böhme must have realized that the heart of new sciences was epistemological and methodological. The issue was a new theory of knowledge, a new epistemology that resulted in a new orientation to things; the new scientists were acquiring an outer knowledge of nature and moving away from an inner knowledge of things. The new knowledge was a certain aloof measuring of things, combined with a pervasive emphasis on a rational analysis of objective facts about nature. Scientific knowledge was (and indeed, still is) an outer knowledge.

To Böhme's, credit he did not reject this knowledge, he simply denied that it provided a comprehensive understanding of life and nature. Böhme saw that this was not a speaking from within or from experience but a speaking from without as spectator, a speaking from a particularly epistemological model. The scientific investigation of nature was a pragmatic means to a useful knowledge.

I argued earlier that the creation of the scientific epistemology and methodology marks the most significant watershed in modern human history. Science has replaced the church as the sole possessor of truth to such an extent that since the nineteenth century, science touts itself as sacred and religion profane. Not only is this is another example of the religious nature and passion behind the scientific enterprise (there are no other truths than those gained through the scientific method), it is also a further conditioning of the pragmatic, calculating consciousness. Because the orientation of science is the only consciousness of value and because this is essentially the pragmatic calculating consciousness made most effective, all other approaches to understanding are sailing a pragmatic course by roping themselves to the scientific ship. The modern world is advancing as if the only valid consciousness is a calculating consciousness.

An alienated modern man, Böhme took to ruminating on a world without God, structure, or meaning. His question was how can we comprehend God and his relationship to nature in a world of infinite space and mechanically moving planets? In a series of mystical intuitions, he received a new understanding of reality. This involved a different conception of God and its relationship to the universe and a new conception of the physical evolution of the universe. Today we call what he did physical and cosmological theory. But, if Böhme's claim to mystical knowledge has validity, his theories were a description of things from an inner approach to reality.

Moreover, because Böhme's mystical insights were precipitated by the doubt and despair the theories of the new sciences implied about God and nature, Böhme's mystically derived inner knowledge of God and the universe was not simply a truth but a prescription for peace of mind. In explaining a new physics and a new vision of God's place in the cosmos, his intuitions defined a solution to the ethotic, meaningless drift of modern life. "Understand what God is, and how his love and wrath have been from eternity, what genesis is and you cannot say that you do not live and be in God, or that God is something foreign to whom you cannot move toward."[14] His assumption was simple: Comprehend creation and you understand life and its relationships. The emptiness, alienation, and distance he experienced were eliminated after he received his insights. In understanding and describing a new physics and a new cosmology, Böhme established a basis for a new ethos. In this sense, Böhme was not simply a post-modern man but a post-modern physicist as well. The stakes were as high for Böhme as they are for Stephen Hawking. Physical and cosmological theory are the basis for any ethos. Naturally, Böhme's ideas contradicted the views founded on the rational outer perspective of Copernican physical and cosmological theory. Böhme's was a cosmological theory born from an inner perspective. Böhme's intuitions proffered not only a different perspective of the universe and God's place in the universe but a redefinition of what the divine being might be. Whereas Galileo envisioned God a mathematician, Böhme saw him as an ever evolving process.

CHAPTER 7

GOD AND NATURE: BÖHME'S MYSTICALLY DERIVED KNOWLEDGE

> There is a thinking in primordial images—in symbols which are older than historical man; which have been ingrained in him from earliest times, and, eternally living, outlasting all generations, [that] still make up the groundwork of the human psyche...wisdom is a return to [these symbols].
>
> C. G. Jung

We accord the designation knowledge only to things that can be verified by repeatable scientific experiment. Speculative descriptions about nature that are recognized as plausible, such as the Big Bang theory, have not been proven conclusively but are interesting because they are part of the historically evolving rationally articulated growth of science; they are recognized as part of the systematic movement of scientific reason toward knowledge. The Big Bang theory is a description of the creation of the universe based on contemporary views on the wave function of the universe, quantum mechanics, and the laws of physics. Additions or deletions to the explanation of how the universe began occur as new theories and new information are collected. The new ideas extend, alter, or confirm the older views. What we consider knowledge or the movement toward knowledge is part of a dynamic ongoing dialogue guided by certain metaphysical assumptions. Knowledge is cumulative.

Descriptions of reality born from a mystical experience are never validated as knowledge because they do not work within or advance the historically conditioned dialogue of humanity. The are outside of time, not within it. When a mystic claims that she or he has acquired a knowledge of nature, she or he is making a claim that says, "I had an immediate intuitive experience that gave me knowledge that was not based on previous experience." A mystical experience cuts across the dialogues that take place within time to provide a knowledge that is outside of time. A mystical claim for knowledge is therefore a bold one.

If there is validity to Böhme's claim for a mystically derived knowledge, the role his rational mind played in these experiences had to have occurred some time after the mystical events, at the point when he went about describing what he was given. The mystical experience itself had to have been, from the perspective of rational activity, a passive-receptive experience. Something was given to him, he did not rationally develop a new addition to the current speculative theories. See Figure 7.1 for a depiction of Moses's mystical experience, receiving divine revelation. Also see Figure 7.2 for an alternate depiction of what mystical knowledge consists of.

As I noted earlier, Böhme supported his claim that he had divine intuitions and had not rationally worked out his theories by insisting that prior to his mystical experiences he was quite ignorant, had "no skill or great understanding," and was "unlearned and a little knowing man, almost childish in comparison to the experienced and the learned." He maintained that his knowledge was not the result of his "reason's work" but rather a "wonder in which God revealed things to him," for he was only a poor simple implement. Böhme wrote down what he experienced and his rambling, chaotic prose certainly lends credence to his assertion that he was poorly educated.

Nonetheless, it is difficult for the modern reader to believe Böhme's knowledge was noncumulative, a message received directly from God. Generally we recognize that we stand on the shoulders of giants. I do not think that there is any doubt that most learning is cumulative, and I have shown that Böhme's own history played a major role in determining, if not his understanding, at least the path he took on his search for knowledge. In a significant way, Böhme's orientation to the world was defined by his history. Still, I am convinced that he had what are called mystical experiences and that they provided him with a unique understanding. He wrote books about what he came to understand during his mystical experiences.

God and Nature

Figure 7.1: The Great Mystery of the World. Note how the angel is lifting Moses's cowl.
Source: The Works of Jacob Böhme. London: M. Richardson, 1764.

TABLE I.	*What* GOD *is without* Nature *and* Creature.			
What God without Nature and Creature is, and what the Mysterium Magnum is: How God, by his Breathing forth or Speaking, has introduced himself into Nature and Creature.		1	Abyss. NOTHING *and ALL*.	
	Father	2	Will of the Abyss,	J E
	Son	3	Delight or Impression of the Will.	H O
	Spirit	4	Science *or* Motion.	V A
		5	GOD in Trinity.	*Thus is* GOD *without* Nature *and* Creature *considered.*
		6	WORD in GOD.	
		7	Wisdom.	

Beginning of Mysterii Magni *of the Eternal* NATURE.						
	GOD *in* LOVE.		GOD *in* WRATH.			
Here begins Mysterium Magnum, *as Distinction in Speaking the* WORD; *where the* WORD *by Wisdom is made distinct, natural, sensible, comprehensible, and invensible.*	8. *The second* V. II. *Angel, Light, Love-Fire.*	Principle. 10. Tincture *or Speaking of the Trinity.*	9. *The First* Principle.			Spiritual Nature, IV. Fire,
			Dark,	Moving, Feeling,	Thinking, Mind,
			I. Desire,	II. Pricking or Science,	III. Anguish,
The eternal Beginning of the Principles is here also understood, with God's Love and Anger, in Light and Darkness.	*Angelical World Root of the four Elements.*	VI. Sound *or Distinction.* VII. *Essence, or essential Wisdom.*	Austere,	Cause *of* Enmity,	Fire Root *of Heat,*	
			Hard,	Hellish Life,	Hell,	Substantial.
	Growing or Greening in the Spiritual World.	12. *Pure Element.* 13. *Paradise.*	Sharpness, cold Fire	Root,	Devil,	
			SAL,	MERCURIUS,	SULPHUR,	

14.	*Beginning of the external* World.		
Here begins the external visible World, as the outspoken visible WORD.	*The third*	Principle.	
1. *Is understood the good Life of the Creature which stands in the Quintessence.*		15. Heaven	
	Stars.	16. Quintessence.	*Good Powers.*
2. *The Poison and Grossness of the Earth and earthly Life.*	*The*	17. *The four Elements.*	*Devil's Poison introduced.*
3. *The Reader understanding these, all Doubts and Queries cease in him; and Babel is left in Ignominy.*	*Out-spoken* WORD.	18. Earthly *Creatures.*	

Figure 7.2: Böhme's view of the evolution of God, Eternal Nature, and the external world (which he also referred to as External Nature).
Source: The Works of Jacob Böhme. London: M. Richardson, 1764.

As noted, a major thrust of this book is that a mystical experience is simply a heightened sense of more common experiences that lead to a certain type of knowledge of reality. These are the experiences that occur to people during those moments when they are not pragmatically but meditatively engaged (gardening, fly-fishing, surfing, snowstorms, random walks, etc.). The understanding that occurs during a mystical experience puts life into perspective and the self at ease. Not easily describable, such experiences are somatosensory connections between us and animals, plants, God, living, and dying. What happened to Böhme was that his somatosensory experiences were intense, long-lasting, frequent, and not curtailed by rational thought. During his mystical experiences, Böhme was not filtering experience through the concepts he had learned about reality. Accordingly, the experiences provided him with an understanding of the existential relationships between things rather than a culturally mediated understanding. The mystical intuitions he had answered the melancholy and despair he felt upon learning about the displacement of God and the destruction of ancient cosmology by the new sciences. They gave him an existential knowledge, a nonrational realization of the connections existing between God, nature, and humanity.

David Hume's arguments against the possibility of knowing anything through reason about God and modern science's experientially based explanation of reality make for a pretty bleak world. A world we cannot argue our way out of. But to assume that the totality of human understanding is subsumed by our rational faculties is to make a serious error. Why restrict experience to the intellectually familiar? The existential knowledge we get while nonpragmatically engaged is a real knowledge, a knowledge that makes us aware of the relationships and connections we live amidst. Mystical knowledge is a deeper awareness of these mysterious interrelationships.

What follows is a description of the knowledge Böhme claimed that he received during his mystical experiences. I chose to mention the Big Bang earlier in the chapter because the heart of Böhme's mystical experiences involved cosmogony: His revelations consisted of a new vision of God's role in the development of the universe, an explanation of the evolution from God of the spiritual forces underlying and leading to creation of the forces underlying corporeal reality, and a vision of how the physical forces of the universe interacted and led to the evolution of nature. This chapter is divided into these three parts of creation as Böhme described them: (1) The evolution of God, (2) the evolution of the spiritual field Eternal Nature, and (3) the spiritual forces that precipitate the evolution of the physical forces behind

External Nature. I have tried to stick as closely as possible to Böhme's descriptions; this makes, at times, for rather dry reading. In chapter 8 I offer my own explanation of what Böhme was describing.

The Growth of God

A fundamental tenet of modern cosmological theory is to define the processes of creation without bringing into account a divine or supernatural force. Modern physics and cosmological theory have striven to define reality under the assumption that a god had nothing to do with it, or, if it did, we cannot talk about it.[1] Indeed, a modern theory of creation would be discredited if a metaphysical element slipped into the explanation. To bring a divine source into a scientific explanation is as much anathema today as to exclude one was 300 years ago. Böhme's vision of the creation of the universe differs from modern theory insofar as it has an original transcendent starting point—God.

This reveals as much, of course, about Böhme's presuppositions about how nature works as the assumption in contemporary efforts of an absolutely natural and neutral physical evolution reveals about the biases of modern science. For Böhme, a conscious entity was and still is involved in creation. During his mystical experiences, Böhme was shown the existence and activity of God. But the experience of God that he received from God was not the fully actualized, omnipotent God of the Pentateuch who orchestrated the creation of the universe in seven days. In *Mysterium Magnum*, a book devoted to discussion of creation, Böhme did not begin to discuss the seven days of creation as described in the Bible until the twelfth chapter. He discussed the seven days of creation only after he had discussed God's creation of Himself and the creation of the inner eternal forces of the universe which would permit the creation of the physical world. His visions involved what came before and made possible the visible, physical universe; they also centered around the evolution of these forces from a God.

Prior to the intuitions, Böhme had acquired a set of historically derived presuppositions about God and creation. Primary among them was a basic Neo-Platonic cosmology. As in Neo-Platonic cosmology, Böhme's conviction was that prior to the original stirrings of a primordial being, there was nothing, or more accurately stated, Nothing existed.

> When I consider what God is, then I say: He is the ONE in reference to all creatures, as an eternal nothing. He has

> neither foundation, beginning or place. He possesses nothing save himself. He is the will of the abyss, he is himself only one. He needs no space or place. He begets himself in himself from eternity to eternity... the eternal wisdom is his delight. He is the will of wisdom. Wisdom is his manifestation.[2]

Elsewhere Böhme stated that God is the "eternal unchanging unity... [It] has nothing, neither before or after It... there is neither ground, time, nor place, but there is only eternal God."[3] To Böhme, the primal nature of God, and therefore the state of the universe prior to God's first efforts, was eternal stillness; the universe was without beginning, being, and time. God was the "Abyss" and the ground of everything (the Byss). "We know that God in his primal essence is not essence, but only naked power, or the understanding to essence as an ungroundable eternal will."[4]

This Neo-Platonic description of primordial being only suggested, as did Aristotle's theories, the base from which all things might originate, it did not explain how God created the universe or how space, time, extension, and being evolved. Böhme's mystical intuitions involved the particulars of that evolution. Böhme was to the Neo-Platonic creation theory what Albert Einstein, Nils Bohr, and Hawking are to the Big Bang.

Böhme's revelations centered around the process by which God moved from eternal no-thing to the creation of the universe, how something could evolve from no-thing (non-being) into the tangible visible world we now inhabit. Böhme was not given an understanding of how an actualized omnipotent being created the universe but an explanation of how God evolved to a point where some-things became possible. This was, I believe, the heart of Böhme's vision: he experienced the process by which God moved from no-thing to some-thing and thereby formed the base of forces from which the universe could evolve. His intuitions involved an explanation of the process of God's self-actualization, and God's creation of the underlying forces of reality. See Figure 7.3 for a traditional rendering of mystical wisdom.

One more point. Böhme did not think that a physical universe of any form was originally in the mind of this primordial God; God was simply "ONE," "wisdom," "will." Thus, if some-thing evolved out of God, it could do so only as God evolved. The issue was that God had to transcend Its eternal state of no-thing (of mere oneness without thingness) if some-thing was to exist. God had to evolve Itself from no-thing into some-thing. Böhme's intuitions told him God did so through the evolution of two trinities: The first involved the manifestation of Itself from ideal unity and no-thing wherein It learned

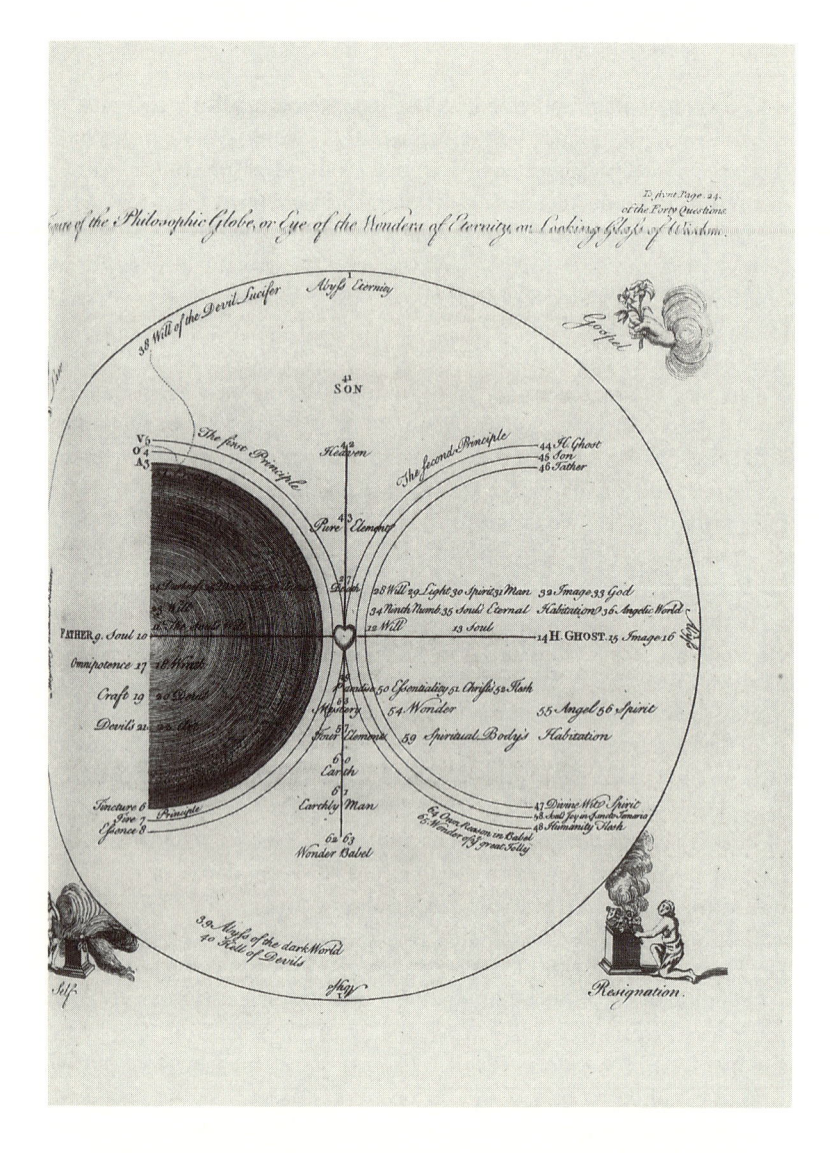

Figure 7.3: The Philosophic Globe or Eye of the Wonders of Eternity:
Diagram of the Glass of Wisdom, frontispiece of 40 Questions.
Source: *The Works of Jacob Böhme.* London: M. Richardson, 1764.

of Its own possibilities, the second involved evolution of those possibilities into actuality.[5]

Whereas modern science attributes the existence of the universe to the Big Bang, Böhme claimed that the event starting things off was a desire, a hunger, a yearning within God. Böhme described this process as "The Nothing hungered after something and the hunger was a desire... the desire had nothing... it conceived itself and impressed itself. It coagulated itself from the Unground into the Ground... and remained still as nothing, it was [at this point] only a quality."[6] Elaborating on this point, Böhme claimed that creation began with an intense desire of God to be some-thing. God wanted to be and that wanting, that desire was the first original fact of the universe. The "desire arose out of the free lubet and made itself out of the free lubet and brought itself into a desire."[7] God became desire. The "desire out of the eternal will of the Unground was the first form and is the FIAT... of everything"[8] The making of that desire was the framing and seeing of desire in God; God became "like an eye"[9] which saw Itself and desired to be filled. God "desired to manifest Itself."[10] Thus, to Böhme, in God and in nature, the conceptual is prior to the physical.

If Böhme believed that desire was the first step of creation, he had in mind a particular form of desire. God's original push towards self-actualization was a curiosity about itself and what it could be. God, according to Böhme, "desired to manifest itself, to fathom itself, and to find out what it was, to bring wonders into being and to reveal itself in the wonders.[11] Stated otherwise, the initial step to the creation was, according to Böhme, the craving for knowledge about self: The impetus for all creation began with the desire for self-consciousness in the eternal being. Thus, God as eternal no-thing, "introduced Itself into Itself in a Lubet in order to see Itself, what It is, and in this Lubet stands wisdom."[12]

But, although the initial process of creation began with the desire for self-consciousness, projection of that original desire outward was necessary for God to perceive Itself. If God had kept that desire within Itself, nothing would have happened. Desire unacknowledged through action remains nothing; God, or at this point, "Pure Desire," needed a mirror to recognize Itself. God needed to act. Action was the mirror whereby God could see and judge Itself. Acting on desire was a further step in the evolution of God and the cosmos. All subsequent events in the universe become the mirror by which God came to know Itself.

From this outward projection of original desire, the elemental forces of reality began. The second stage of creation was the evolution of the properties (or forces) sometimes called by Böhme, "qualities," "forms," or "spirits."[13] These properties were the result of how God, the immense abyssal eternal understanding, manifested Itself.[14] Böhme claimed that there were seven properties. The evolution of these seven properties from eternal nothing established the realm of reality Böhme called Eternal Nature. Before physical temporal reality could be formed, Eternal Nature (the spiritual eternal field and forces of reality) evolved. Böhme named the seven properties and attributed to them the following characteristics:

> Desire—astringent, contracting
> Bitter—attractive, expansive
> Anguish—perceiving, feeling
> Fire—spirit, reason
> Light—love
> Sound—word, natural understanding
> Essence—house

Böhme was clear that the properties were not physically real, although they were that from which the forces behind nature emerged. They were not chemical reactions nor subatomic reactions. To Böhme, they were simply the properties or qualities underlying and making possible physical forces of nature. They were the original source of novelty.[15] As such, they were the eternal multipossible internal forces that formed the foundation and precipitated the movement of all reality. Böhme's properties were the elementary forces of life, not life itself but the fundamental forces from which life originated and continues to evolve. "Nature stands in its first ground in the seven properties which divide themselves endlessly."[16] Böhme was also quick to caution that the seven properties were not separate but all one, a group. They were not "seven divided qualities, one against the other ... [but] all seven are one, and no one of them is first or last, the last is first."[17] According to Böhme, there was not one elementary force behind reality but seven; but all seven make up one force.[18] A field of independent eternal forces established the basis of reality. Each individual property works against each other but together they form a unified force-field.

As stated above, creation of the seven properties began with God's desire to be. With the initiation of this desire a tension began—God's original desire became the first property because that desire created a conflict within God. In seeking to satisfy the desire a tension was created. As God sought to be more than it was, the original desire became "astringent, harsh, impressing sizing itself ... and [it] made the great darkness of the abyss."[19] This was a contracting force; the desire pulled God back into itself; the "pulling in of the desire is a stinging hardness of movement."[20] This led to the second quality which, reacting against the contraction, forces itself outward, moving against the contraction of the first force. The second quality was an opposition to the contraction.

This was the second major insight Böhme had about an evolving and expansive universe: The universe evolved dialectically. Conflict, as expansive and contracting processes, undergirds all living activity. Evolution involved a dialectical process based on an original "enmity between the bitterness or hardness and the sting of the hardness," just as an inner desire is countered by an inner reaction.[21] To Böhme, such contractions and the expansions were not two different forces but different aspects derived from or included in the original force. Often he described them as the love and hate existing in the same individual; they were a dialectically active and interactive entity, a vibrating source of activity exactly because they were opposing forces.

> It is like a father and son: the father wants to be quiet and hard, but the stinging of the son seeks the father and causes unrest. This causes the father who cannot suffer the bitterness to seek more vigorously in himself to stop the disobedient son... then the son will become stronger in his attacks [and the process continues].[22]

The evolving of this dialectic of being created a third property. Böhme described this property as an "anguish or torment or source which the first two properties made."[23] This property was a coming into feeling or into sensibility, the growth of self-consciousness or feeling. The conflict of the first two qualities precipitated the "out-breaking of the first feeling and the beginning of essence."[24]

> [Contraction against expansion precipitates anguish and] the bitter desire grasps itself and looks into itself and makes itself full, hard and cold; so is the pull [the second property] an enemy of the harshness. The harshness is stopped and the pulling is retreated. One wants [to go] out of himself, but they cannot yield to one another or divide themselves, so they will go into one another like a third wheel.[25]

A result of this feeling or perception was the creation of the fourth property. This property Böhme called Fire because the will is made volatile by understanding and perception. The fourth property was a "spiritual fire wherein the light that is a unity is made manifest."[26] Böhme also saw this property as a connecting link between the first set of three properties and the succeeding three. The fifth property was the light given off by the fire of the fourth property. Here was the "world of fire and love."[27] The sixth property was the "Eternal Sound" or understanding because "when the fire flashes all the properties sound together." Here all the properties understand each other."[28] They are like a tone, a voice, a sound originating out of all the others.[29] Böhme also called this property a "melody as if the mind played in a kingdom of joy with itself."[30]

The seventh property was the introduction of the first six into "eternal essence." This was the point at which all the properties "pass their love play into a form."[31] The six previous properties have congealed or become active forces; they are, as a group, an entire new level of potentiality. They are now separated or somewhat distinct from God. From the sum of the parts a whole is created which encompasses the parts but is greater than them. The snake has bitten it tail, turned around itself and become a circle of potentiality.[32]

This new level of potentiality was necessary so that the previous properties "might have something in which and with which to continue their wrestling love-play."[33] The new level was not a tangible substance, but sort of a spiritual clay; it formed the realm which permitted a new and continual process of divine manifestation to occur but it was not itself physical. Spiritual water was the "framed essence of the properties, a manifestation of the powers: what the first six were in spirit the seventh was in comprehensible essence, as a house of all the rest, or as a body of the spirit wherein the spirit worked and played with itself."[34]

The seven properties together formed an invisible intangible realm of possibility, a new level of spiritual being a field of manifested power. According to Böhme, this field was a place wherein the mind of Godly revelation could behold Itself in time and play with Itself. It was within this field that the properties mixed and battled with each other, forming the eternal field of force from which everything originated. Opposites—love/hate, bitter/sweet, and so on—were set up by Böhme as contrasting but conjugal. Opposites precipitate life, but opposites are not distinct separate entities—they are part of the same whole.[35]

Böhme's conception of the actualization of the processes by which the primordial being spreads itself out is through a series of conflicting couplings or contrasting forces that produce a third force. The process is dialectal: one force conflicts with another to form a third. The scheme might be conceived as such:

> Step 1. God, containing within or generating within Force A.
> Step 2. Simultaneously there is a reaction, Force B.
> Step 3. Forces A and B conflict and form Force C.
> Step 4. Force C contains within it Forces D and E.
> Step 5. Forces D and E conflict and form Force F.
> Step 6. The sum of Forces A, B, C, D, E, and F as a whole form a level of Being, G.

The Evolution of Eternal Nature into the Spiritual Forces

This was not the end of Böhme's explanation of the growth of the cosmos. The properties that had evolved out of and within God had indeed formed. When combined, a new level of being existed, something other than God. Böhme called this level of being Eternal Nature, the spiritual ground or field of force from which all future forms of life evolved.

In its original form, Eternal Nature was only a mass, a "spiritual water" wherein the seven properties play. At this point, Böhme envisions the universe (Eternal Nature) as having no particularity, it is merely the eternal potential force from which particularity might originate. Böhme then went on to describe and account for the rise of particular spiritual invisible forces from within Eternal Nature. What he was concerned with discussing at this point was the intermediary forces between Eternal Nature and the physical forces underlying the physical reality we are and experience. He believed that the "outward world with the four elements and stars was a figure of the internal powers of the spiritual world,"[36] and his vision accounted for the creation of the powers derived from the original force-field that initiated what we are and experience. Eternal Nature, the field of forces that lay at the base of creation, now existed. The next aspect of Böhme's revelation consisted of a vision of how this field of force evolved even further. The issue? What connected Eternal Nature to External Nature?

Böhme's answer was that there was a further development of Eternal Nature, an outgoing or outward movement from the general field to particularity. This movement was the "outward heaven, the powers of the water: the word FIAT, which began with the beginning of the world now became filled."[37] From the base of Eternal Nature, outer, external spiritual forces formed. This level of forces contained such things as Paracelsus's three principles, the four elements, the Holy Ghost, and the spiritual aspects of the stars and the sun.

All these forces were invisible but effective, and Böhme's description of how particular spirituality developed from within Eternal Nature is just as confusing as his explanation of the growth of External Nature. Nevertheless, the process itself is similar and involves the seven properties in a continuing series of dialectical relationships that result in the evolution of the possibility for particularity. In this description there is, again, expanding and contracting imagery, bitter/sweet, love/hate conflicts, and a seven-step process.

Böhme also maintained the principle from his earlier explanation that although this was a movement toward the particular, the particular was not less than the whole. Every unique thing contained all the spiritual forces that came before it in addition to its own particularity. The life-actuating spiritual forces of salt were specific aspects of Eternal Nature but they were also all that Eternal Nature was. Thus, within each one of these new forces was contained all seven properties of nature derived from God's earlier evolution plus a new particularity. Moreover, when Böhme discussed the four elements (à la Aristotle), the sun, moon, or the Paracelsian principles, he believed that each one of these forces also contained the unique qualities of each other. "In each element lies a whole Astrum."[38] Yet each one was a unique force. To Böhme, the seven properties

> Make in the internal world the holy element, namely the holy natural life and motion, but this one element severs itself in the external world into four manifest properties, the four elements, yet it is only one but divides itself into four head springs.[39]

What Böhme envisioned was a unity between all the realms of nature and God. The outer (but still an invisible spiritual substance) contained all the powers of the original development of Eternal Nature and yet was original and new. Conceptually speaking, Böhme's vision was of the continual expansion of the primal forces God had unleashed in his first act of will and idea, God moving outward in ever more sophisticated expression. "The outer is an image of the inner. God is nothing unfamiliar, in him live and move all things but each according to its own principle and degree."[40] The entire realm of spiritual forces would interact, converge, and live according to and based on the original properties, but individual particularity was also present. Böhme summed up his vision in the following general statement.

Each kind is created out of many things, each out of a different degree, and each kind lives in its mother [spiritual] when it has originated as the beasts upon the earth... for the Fiat extracted them out of the earth's property... the birds were created out of the sulfur of the air therefore they fly in their mother... and each lives in its mother where it was taken in the beginning and the contrary is death.[41]

The Evolution of External Nature

Only after discussing what he called the eternal and internal forces of creation did Böhme concern himself with the evolution of physical matter, or, in his terminology, the *Seven Days of Creation*. To Böhme, the Seven Days has far greater significance than the mere creation of the visible universe as described in Genesis. His insights dealt with, once again, the inner forces leading to the creation of the universe. The Biblically stated days are recognized by Böhme to be another step in the series of separations that continue the events originated by God's initial desire. To Böhme, the days of creation were the evolution of the field of force called the seven properties into physical form. Thus, "the seven days work have a far more subtle meaning than length of time, for the seven properties are also understood therewith."[42] He describes the Seven Days as follows:

First Day: The first motion of the word which equals light enkindling itself to essence.

Second Day: The movement of the eternal heavenly essence into the external heavenly essence, wherein the soul of the outward world works.

Third Day: The establishment of the (actual) [Paracelsian] principles. This is senseless life within the three principles, a moving growing life.

Fourth Day: The beginning of sensing life, the feeling life in the three principles and the four elements. Here the astrum became manifest in fire, air, earth, and water. Tangible reality, outward nature is formed.

Fifth Day: The creatures are produced in all four elements in earth, each according to its own properties: the birds in the air, fish in the water, beasts on the earth, and the spirits in fire.

Sixth Day: Jovial powers are created; fire-love, the desire in which each life longs after its likeness and longs to procreate

Seventh Day: The whole of the previous six properties are herein contained. All potential possibilities have been set in motion.[43]

Because Böhme viewed creation as an expanding continuum, the Seven Days are God evolving into extension in space and duration in time. Corporeal reality is the result of the "six properties of the active life having introduced and manifested themselves out of the inward spiritual world into an external visible world of four elements."[44] Temporal and spatial reality is the spiritual forces of the universe taking the possibilities available to them and manifesting them into visible form or image. The earth is the "gross out-flowing of this subtle world ... it originated out of the ground as from the Spiritus Mundi which has its root in the inner world."[45] Böhme went on to say that "we are to understand nothing else by the creation than that the Verbum Fiat had amassed the spiritual birth and introduced it into a visible external domain and essence."[46]

However, despite the fact that everything was connected to God, the result of the process, the Seventh Day, was a distinct entity. The corporeal world was a new realm of being: The Seventh Day is a "house of the working life, wherein [spatial-temporal reality] stands as a figure to the contemplation of the great glory of God."[47] To Böhme, the tangible state of things—past and present nature and its current relationship to spirit and God—is the Seventh Day. The Seventh Day is the present state of things as they evolved from the original stirrings of the divine urge. We are in the Seventh Day of the evolution of things that reflect God.

CHAPTER 8

AN INNER VIEW OF THINGS

What can we say about these bitter/sweet, good/evil conflicts that Böhme claimed are inherent in nature? What can we say about the images of God as desire, as striving, as imagination? About astringency, love and hate, and good and evil as inherent forces in nature? About the Seventh Day as stage a in the evolution of God? This is all rather primitive.[1] Is this part of the mythic mind, part of the organically inspired natural view of reality, something that should be left behind as an earlier and inferior mode of prerational consciousness?[2] Perhaps. But it is also possible that what Böhme experienced and the knowledge he acquired from those experiences reflects a mode of consciousness that although no longer common, has validity, that it is not something earlier, lower, and inferior to rational pragmatic consciousness, something inadequate and inferior, but something different.

Mystical experience is a mode of consciousness that provides an alternate explanation reality; an autochthonic state of human consciousness resulting in an existential level of understanding. What follows is my attempt to put Böhme's statements into comprehensible form.

Böhme's View of the Creation

Böhme's vision of creation involved a three-step evolutionary process. Working from the broad to the particular, we get the following:

I. God, the Eternal No-Thing, as pure conceptuality and possibility evolves into possibility, thereby initiating the seven forms. The forms are the primal properties or forces of reality generated from God's original desire to explore possibilities. They are the foundation of the forces that will evolve into the spiritual field Eternal Nature.

II. Eternal Nature is a field of spiritual forces. Evolving within and as part of Eternal Nature are specific spiritual properties. The properties are the forces generating uniqueness into External Nature.

III. External Nature is both the physical forces underlying tangible reality and tangible reality. As the former, it is the force underlying the change and evolution of nature. As the latter, it is the nature we are and experience.

Each of these realms is separate yet connected; each is an independent self-contained entity with its own specific set of forces; yet each is part of the preceding as well as the existing whole. The overriding conception is one of uniqueness within unity. For Böhme, the primal force of life—God—extended outward as a series of forces. "There is a life and a spiritual government in the deep of the world in all places so that all the creatures are included as it were in one body."[3] "One quality goes into another, because they are all from one, as flowing from the free joy. Therefore the same joy is in everything and each wishes to go again into the same free joy. Everything affects one another in their holy conjunction."[4] The overriding conceptual understanding Böhme derived from his mystical experiences was that creation entailed a series of interconnected evolving steps. See Figures 8.1 and 8.2, graphical representations of Böhme's vision of creation—the evolution of some-thing from no-thing.

The first realm of this expansive system involved the evolution of the primal forces of movement that would account for or be fundamental to all continued development. The second realm, a spiritual nonphysical field, generated the possibility of the forces of physical reality. This realm of spiritual forces is different from the physical forces modern science studies. The physics of modern science would be similar to Böhme's third realm, the forces governing his External Nature. As I read him, Böhme would, at some level, agree with modern science that the outer world of objects was governed by the smaller inner realm of atomic matter; he would differ from the modern view insofar as he claims that there is an inner spiritual field of forces that influences atomic and subatomic matter.

The process of creation can be seen as a separation from God. In this sense, Böhme echoed his Paracelsian and Neo-Platonic heritage. However, Böhme's vision was more of a concentric process exploding from a divine center, forever enlarging the original. Similar to

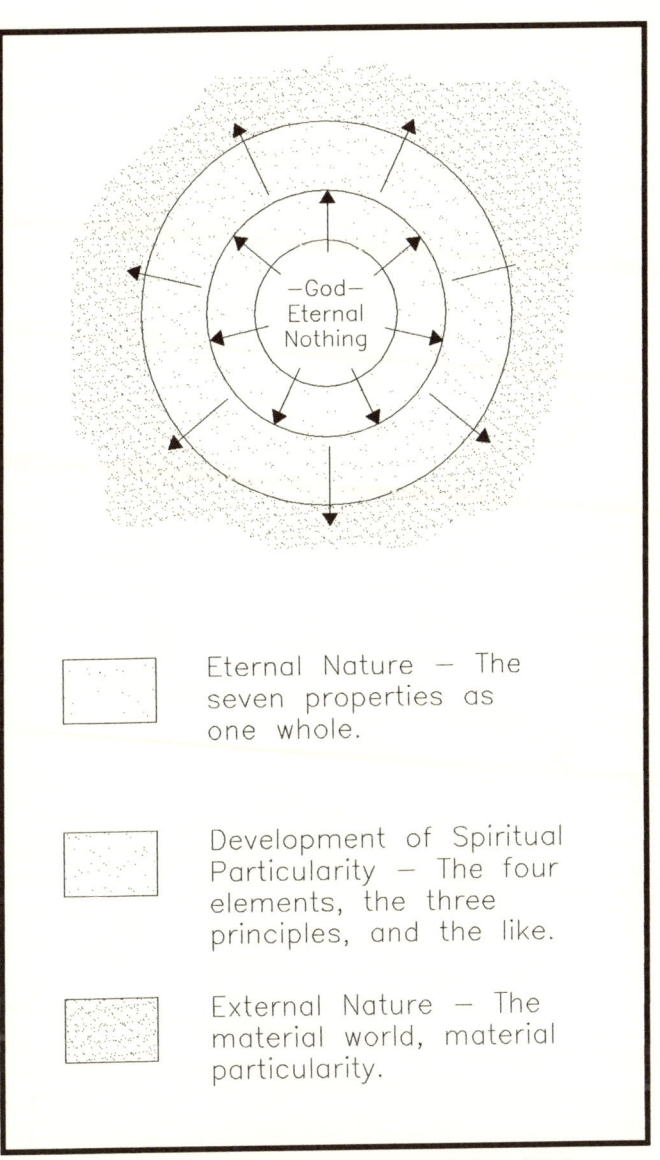

Eternal Nature — The seven properties as one whole.

Development of Spiritual Particularity — The four elements, the three principles, and the like.

External Nature — The material world, material particularity.

Figure 8.1: Böhme's vision of the evolution of God from no-thing to some-thing.

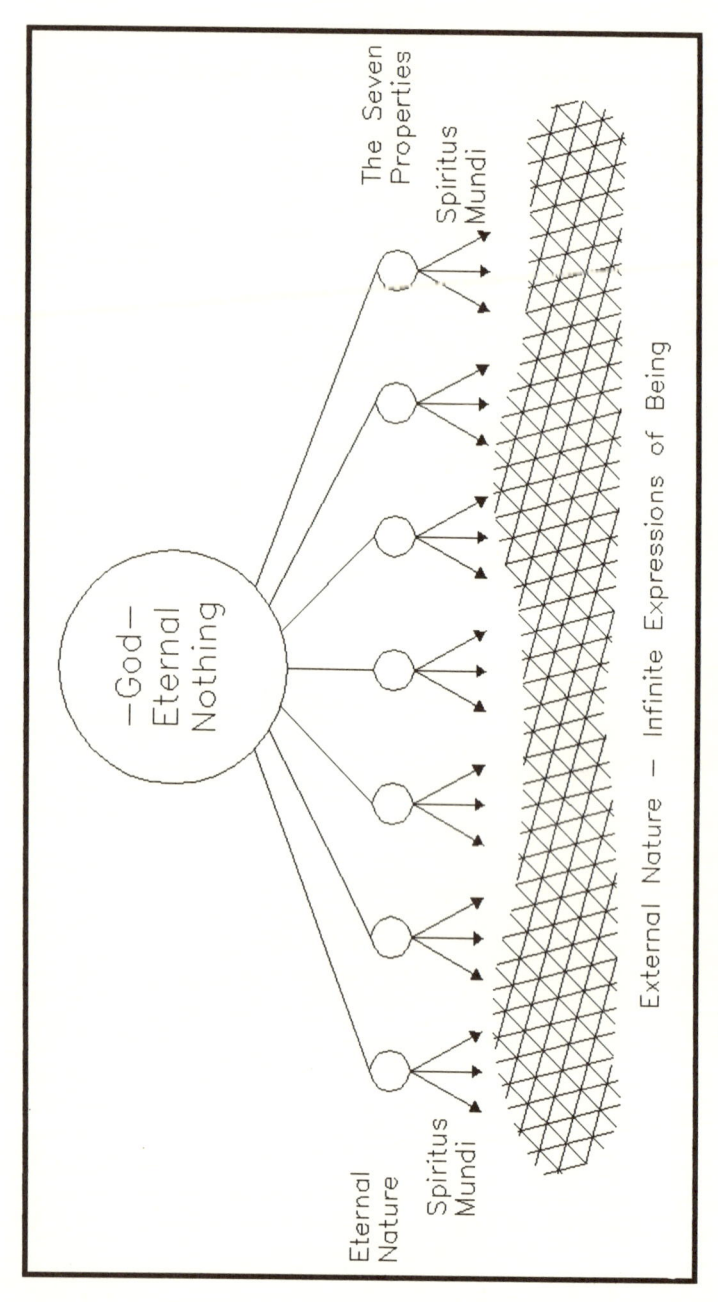

Figure 8.2: Böhme's vision of the evolution of God from no-thing to some-thing.

Aristotle's vision in *De Anima*, in Böhme's vision, life started from within and moved outward in expansive development of being—the "Godhead is like a wheel." The vision was that of a process of increasing particularization and perfection of primal being, not separation from primal being. Böhme's cosmological scheme is evolutionary, not creationist, as Paracelsus held. Life proceeded from the less perfect to the more perfect. Böhme's cosmogony contradicted, as his own vision of life contradicts, the neoclassical notion of a static universe in which an earlier state of perfection existed. From potential whole particularity ensues; each entity contains the original forces and properties, it is part of the original continuum and is therefore expansion of primordial being.

The process may be seen from another perspective—a whole God encompassing everything and creation moving inward toward particular levels of expression. This idea is not contradictory, but complementary. The spreading outward of the first image is simultaneously a turning inward because of the God-world continuum.

God

Böhme's vision of God differs from than the traditional Judeo-Christian version in several ways. Here there is no kingly being snapping his fingers to create the universe, no omnipotent ruler of what takes place, no teleological guidance. There is no final stage of absolute perfection, with Caesar looking down on the imperfect changelings far below. Böhme's God was not omnipotent.

Creation of the universe began with God and continues to involve God as primordial initiator: The primal being, dissatisfied with eternal nothing, instilled desire into himself and a force was initiated. God was the start of an energy forces from which everything else evolved. "The birth of the earth stands in its original as the whole deity does and there is no difference at all...all the seven spirits of God are in the earth and generate as they do in heaven for the earth is in God and God never died."[5] Only God, as Eternal Nothing, ground and unground, is independent of prior forces.

But God is dependent on all that comes forth from It for advancement of Its own self-consciousness. Creation and expansion of the universe is change and expansion of God. God becoming self-conscious is the initiating force of the universe. Since the universe represents the eternal properties of nature becoming manifest, nature is the spiritual, physical, and corporeal movement of God. Nature is a mirror of God. "He dwells in nothing but Himself and yet He lives through all things; He is not far off nor near anything, but God is the expressed world, the formed word."[6] Change is evolving creative process. "God gave Himself something, and took that something again into Himself and gave another out. He introduced Himself to joy and desire for the purpose of power, strength, and virtue, and led Himself from one level to another." When asked why God manifested Itself, Böhme replied, "There is no other reason than that He Himself [wanted] to introduce the spiritual world into a visible pictured Form so that the inner powers will be pictured and formed."[7]

Böhme's vision of God's relationship to the universe would seem to imply some sort of pantheism. But Böhme held that this was not the case. God provoked the possibility of life, and some aspects of the initial energy and forces he unleashed were contained in every object, but God was not that life itself. God was no more a plant or a tree than the inventor is her or his invention, a bird is its nest, or Mr. and Mrs. Smith are their children. No tangible thing—stone, tree, or human—is God.

> We cannot say the outward world is God ... likewise that the outward man is God; things are only the expressed word which has coagulated itself in its conception to its own expression and does still coagulate itself with the four elements.[8]

Nature might be the striving actuality of the process of God's original manifestation, but the soul is not God itself. God is neither the forces precipitating nature nor nature. All nature is part of the whole, and each entity possesses all the conflicting potentialities initiated by God by virtue of it being part of the continuum initiated by God. The universe is to God as inventions are to inventors, nests to birds, and children to parents.

Nature

The motif of imagination, desire, and the will to create that Böhme saw God as initiating continued in his description of nature, producing similar tensions and conflicts. Indeed, nature is conflict and conflict is a force of evolution. To Böhme, conflict is inherent in the evolving processes of the universe in two ways: There is an individual mental component and there is opposition from the entities resisting being impinged upon. About the latter, it was obvious to Böhme that "there was an enmity between heat and cold and they are never at one."[9] "Each quality gives forth from itself into the others and stirs the other, affecting it."[10] To Böhme, everything in nature was in conflict; always there is "war and contention, a building and breaking."[11] Life draws fruitfulness from the earth and then in turn is destroyed or swallowed up again.

> In the earth you cannot perceive anything besides the herbs, plants or vegetables and metals more than astringency, bitterness and water. The water is now sweet, opposite to the other two qualities, it is thin and the other two are hard, and always one against the other. There is a perpetual struggling, fighting, and wrestling, and herein lies the source of change.[12]

> Conflict is in all creatures, and also in each body itself...but not only in living bodies, but also in stars and elements, earth, rocks, metals, in wood, leaves, and grass: in everything is poison and evil.[13]

The original creation and subsequent evolution of things was not the result of molecules blindly bouncing off one another to lead (like the mythical monkeys who produce *Hamlet* by randomly pounding typewriter keys) to the great work of nature. There is a mental element in evolution. Böhme attributes prefiguring consciousness to the spiritual level of nature, the "deep between the earth and the stars, is like the minds of men who see something and will to create it and then bring it into essence."[14] Hence, nature has imagination insofar as it imagines its possibilities in the same way God did. Imagination, initiated by God and evolving through the three levels of reality, is part of the force that helps to produce novelty. Imagination leads to desire, desire is tension, and this leads to conflict, leads to possibility, leads to the movement to achieve, to change, to evolve. In this way, Böhme accounts for those creative jumps in the evolutionary process (e.g., from no-thing to some-thing, from the inorganic to the organic, from the organic to the mental) as something more than accident.

There is a grasping, striving mind behind evolution. Not a mind that knows in advance what it wants to do and then does, but a thinking mind that evolves within and from the possibilities currently open to it. This is true for individual entities too. Each entity, within its range of possibilities, possesses potentiality and can imagine itself forward. The images and possibilities are determined by its own state and the environmental conditions encountered.

But this picture of the imaginary potential inherent in creation is incomplete. Böhme's cosmology suggests a dual conception of the mental activity that underlies and takes place in the evolutionary process—the pure mental activity of thought whereby possibilities are envisioned and the mental activity wherein the envisioned possibilities are developed.[15] It was the purely conceptual visions that Böhme was concerned with describing in his explanation of the movement of God from nothing to something. At this level, the level of potentiality and possibility, there were only properties. The properties (essentially, yearning ideas) were devoid of empirical content. The second mental level was the idea put to into form. The physical result of the primal yearnings was never perfect; the reality reached was never the original ideal. The ideal plane is hardly imaginable: An idea makes form possible and form is an evolving representation of an idea, but neither idea nor form are perfect. That is why God, life, the universe, and everything is always in process. The impurity of the concretized idea, the differences among trees, among rocks, and among humans that make up the temporal sphere does not negate the fact that only as a process is God and nature made more perfect. As Böhme clearly saw, the world was not perfect, but it was fighting to become so.

There was no other way for God to visualize Itself. God is not in complete control. God did not allow or start the Holocaust. God does not permit babies to die. God is part of a process. Not an unconscious part but an envisioning part. God is an imagining entity that sets forth possibilities of moving toward perfection but who, because of the fundamental nature of creation as oppositional and evolutionary, lacks complete control. God is a moving part of an evolving process. The evolution of the universe is toward higher states, but the road there was not laid out in advance. In Böhme's scheme, God is building the road in order to take the next step.

Creation was and remains an evolutionary process.[16] Perhaps this was Böhme's most significant understanding. The universe was not a static system but an open and evolving one. Teleology was not part of Böhme's conception. Individuals are on their own, chance is a part of the universe. God is not in complete control of the forces unleashed by Its original desire. According to Böhme, nature was causal and sequential but also creative, willful, evolving, imagined, and sought; it was not determined.

Böhme's revelation showed him that antinomies and contradictions were inherent in reality and that a proper interpretation of reality incorporated such ideas. God *did* play dice to Böhme and, moreover, the die themselves were alive. They also hated each other and there was really only one of them, but they fought all the time. Not only that, they were always changing their shapes, but they were always the same. And every time they came together a new thing emerged. It was a new game all the time, but it was always the same old game. It was the game of life that Böhme was involved in describing, and his understanding of that game was really what an inner understanding gives people.

NOTES

CHAPTER 1

1. My limited understanding of how the brain works was derived in part from Antonio R. Damasio, *Descartes' Error* (New York: Putnam, 1994).

2. This point has been made over and over again but most recently by Paul Davies, *The Mind of God: The Scientific Basis for a Rational World* (New York: Touchstone, 1992). The nature of the experience of science is discussed in more detail in chapter one.

3. I recognize that understanding and controlling nature are two different things and that there is a difference between pure and applied science. But whereas pure science emphasizes understanding how nature works, the roots and history of science since the seventeenth century have been encompassed by the desire for power and control of nature.

4. Interestingly, Schopenhauer (not to mention Nietzsche), the ultimate sceptic, presented a more balanced view of the religious than Freud's rather one-sided condemnation. Arthur Schopenhauer, *Religion: A Dilogue* (New York: Arno Press, 1972, reprint 1891 edition).

5. Although the majority of criticisms about how science and technology have destroyed the world are trivial, there is an element of truth in them. The success of the scientific epistemological and methodological practices in supplying an understanding of nature and leading to control of nature has led to a furthering of the useful project of humanity and a gradual closing off of anything that smacks of the nonuseful. Science did not close off religious activity, but its success

has led to the possibility of more and more people being able to engage with and be successful in the useful. Science itself, because it requires the adoption of a particular set of metaphysical beliefs, is a religion. The decline of morality has less to do with the denial of religion by science—the values of science state specifically to ignore religion—and more to do with the lack of fear on the part of more and more people to simply engage in the useful rather than the religious.

6. According to polls taken since 1944, the percentage of Americans believing in God has averaged about ninety-six percent. The percentage of Europeans believing in God is much lower but still well above fifty percent. Information taken from Frank J. Tipler, *The Physics of Immortality: Modern Cosmology, God, and the Resurrection of the Dead* (New York: Doubleday, 1995), 345-8.

7. I discuss the relationship between brain, minds, langauge, and feeling in greater detail in chapter five.

8. Haigiographic legend has it that he was totally isolated and inspired by the holy spirit to write the book. By happenstance, a nobleman, von Ender, entered his shop and while waiting for his shoes glanced over the text, became excited, borrowed it, and discovered a great author. Peuckert and others have shown this to be false. Will-Erik Peuckert, "Das Leben Jacob Böhme" in *Jacob Böhme, Sämtliche Schriften* (Stuttgart: Fr. Frommann's Verlag, 1961), Vol. 10.

9. Georg Wilhelm Friedrich Hegel, *Werke*. Vol. 3: "Vorlesungen über die Geschichte der Philosophie." (Stuttgart: FR. Frommann's Verlag, 1932). Ludwig Feuerbach, *Vorlesungen über die Geschichte der neueren Philosophie* (Darmstadt: Wissenschaftlich Buchgesellschaft, 1956) also spent time on Böhme.

10. Such statements are a refrain in Böhme's writings, but see especially, Jacob Böhme, "Briefe" in *Jacob Böhme's Sämtliche Schriften*. Ed. Will-Erick Peuckert (Stuttgart: Fr. Frommanns Verlag, 1961), letters 10 and 11. All quotations from Böhme in this book are from this edition and will be defined after notation by the short title of the work.

CHAPTER 2

1. Hans-Georg Gadamer, *Truth and Method* (New York: Seabury Press, 1977), develops this point in great detail.

2. Benjamin L. Whorf, "Thinking in Primitive Communities," in *New Directions in the Study of Language* (New York: Hoyer Editions, 1964) described this as "We dissect nature along lines laid down by our native languages...the world is presented in a kaleidoscopic flux of

impressions which has to be organized by our minds. We cut nature up, organize into concepts ... largely because we are parties to an agreement to organize it in this way—an agreement that holds throughout our speech community and is codified in the pattersn of our language ... we cannot talk at all except by subscribing to the organization and classsification of data which the agreement decrees," 23.

3. See Timothy Reiss, *The Discourse of Modernism* (Ithaca, NY: Cornell University Press, 1982). Reiss describes the discourse of modernism as an "'analytic-referential' class of discourse ... [that] became the single dominant structure and the necessary form taken by thought, by knowledge, by cultural and social practices of all kinds," 23.

4. Galileo Galilei, "Letter to the Grand Duchesse" in *Discoveries and Opinions of Galileo* (New York: Doubleday, 1957) and *Dialogue on the Two Chief World Systems* (Berkeley: University of California Press, 1967). Both are rhetorical masterpices. The first argues that the Copernican theory is true and that its truths do not contradict the truths of the Scriptures when they are "rightly understood" (179-80). Galileo goes on to limit the sphere of knowledge the Scriptures offer to those things that cannot be grasped by a scientific investigation of nature (197). The *Dialogue*, an attempt to prove that the events happening on a moving Earth would be no different than those occuring on a stationary Earth, continually ridicules the simple Aristotelian approach to the study of nature.

5. More illustrative is the difference between anatomy texts of the Middle Ages and Vasalius' 1543 *De Frabrica*. During the Middle Ages, the anatomical approach was untutored, direct. The physician cut open the body and began the examination. Vasalius divided the body into systems (muscular, cardiovascular, etc.) and devised a systematic set of steps to follow when analyzing the body.

6. Francis Bacon outlined in 1620 the problem of acquiring truth in the face of various sociocultural biases. He called the prejudices that get in the way of truth the "Idols of the Mind." See *The New Organon*, Ed. Fulton H. Anderson (New York: Bobbs-Merrill, 1960), sections 38-62.

7. *Newton's Philosophy of Nature*. Selections, Ed. H. S. Thayer (New York: Hafner Press, 1974), 17-25.

8. Gadamer 1977, 433.

9. René Descartes, "Meditations on First Philosophy" in *Philosophical Works*, (Cambridge: Cambridge University Press, 1978), 185.

10. Reiss 1982, 30.

11. Michael Polanyi, *Personal Knowledge* (Chicago: University of Chicago Press, 1962), 3-4. Polanyi's critique of the "objective" and "critical thinking" claims of modern science is as stimulating today as it was when printed. Scientific truths are not divorced from the human because of the establishment of theory as more important than sense experience. Science simply abandoned the "crude anthropomorphism of our senses...in favor of a more ambitious anthropomorphism of our reason," 4-5.

12. Galileo 1967, 145-6.

13. Bacon 1960, 22.

14. Werner Heisenberg, *Across the Frontiers*. (New York: Harper, 1974), 215.

15. Ibid., 216.

16. Gadamer 1977, 258.

17. Herein lies the importance of reading. Reading is not simply a language activity, it is a neurological one as well. Reading conditions neuroligcal patterns within the brain. It is like lifting weights: the more deeply and seriously one reads the more developed become one's linguistically based powers.

18. Gadamer 1977, 463.

19. Ibid., 317.

20. George Steiner, *Real Presences* (Chicago: University of Chicago Press, 1989). Gadamer (1977) makes a similar point in "Language as Horizon of the Hermeneutic Ontology," 438-91.

21. Bertrand Russell, *Mysticism and Logic*, (New York: Doubleday, 1957), 14-5.

22. I paraphrase Gadamer (1977, 449) here.

23. Hans Peter Duerr, *Dreamtime*, Trans. Felicitas Goodman (New York: Basil Blackwell, 1985), 85.

24. Robert Musil, *Precision and Soul* (Chicago: University of Chicago Press, Ed. and Trans. Burton Pike and David S. Luft, 1990), 199.

25. See Philip Novak, "Attention," *The Encyclopedia of Religion*, Ed. Mircea Eliade (New York: Macmillan, 1987).

CHAPTER 3

1. William James, *The Varieties of Religious Experience* (New York: Collier Books, 1961), 300. James' study of mysticism is interesting because, aside from his analytical efforts, the basis of his understanding was a drug-induced experience. James claims that his experiences on nitrous oxide made him aware that "our normal waking

consciousness, rational consciousness as we call it, is but one special type of consciousness, whilst all about it, parted from it by the filmiest of screens, there lie potential forms of consciousness entirely different," 305.

2. Martha Heyneman, "The Never-Ceasing Dance." in *Parabola*. (Summer 1991): 6.

3. Philip Novak, "The Practice of Attention." *Parabola*. (Summer 1990), 10.

4. Böhme, *Briefe*, 11, par. 8.

5. Novak 1990, 11-12.

6. Damasio 1994, 128.

7. What I describe is not new. St. Thomas Aquinas outlined the basic mechanics of thought and how the distorting effects of imagery distanced individuals from the reality they were describing through concepts.

8. In this suggestion I have taken Damasio's (1994) reading of how the mind works and applied it. I am not sure Mr. Damasio would agree with my leaping off from his views into the realms of mysticism, but certainly, if there is any truth to the statements of mystics, they would have to take place between us and an event, between self and other. I am assuming that mystical experiences are a more primordial level of existence, more of an immediate existential event than the more evolved, mentally conditioned and evaluated experiences we normally have. One of the points Damasio makes involves the physical aspects of this process in terms of the "old" part of the brain and the "new." It is in the old part of the brain, the hypothalamus and brain stem, that the body is regulated, and this section of the brain needs to be intact for the higher levels of thought to occur. It is in the "modern and experience-driven sectors of the brain (e.g., the neocortex) ... that the neural representation on which mind (images) and mindful actions are based. But the neocortex cannot produce images if the old-fashioned subterranean of the brain (hypothalamus, brain stem) is not intact and cooperative," 110.

9. Damasio 1994, 240.

10. Ibid., 240.

11. Ibid., 243.

12. James 1962, 302.

13. Arthur Deikman, *Bimodal Consciousness and the Mystic Experience*, 73.

14. Ibid., 75

15. Damasio 1994, 150-55.

16. Böhme, *Aurora*, chap. 20, par. 10-13.

17. Böhme, *Briefe*, 12, par. 10.
18. Böhme, *Aurora*, chap. 19, par. 14.

CHAPTER 4

1. Friedrich Nietzsche, see "Notes," in *The Portable Nietzsche*, Ed. and Trans. Walter Kaufmann (New York: Penguin, 1968), 455.

2. Psychotherapy of one type or another works, I believe, only when the rational configurations the individual has acquired are undermined and another comprehension becomes realized, dimly at first but eventually more clearly. Successful treatments in psychotherapy have to do with destroying mental precepts that precipitated neurotic habits of thought and returning the individual to a more original state of being. Ultimately, the brain reconfigures itself. Freudian talk on the couch is less about the talk than it is about the loss of structured thought through random talk. The point is to get through the conscious screens to the latent and presently unconscious experience.

3. Gerhart B. Ladner, *The Idea of Reform.* (Cambridge: Cambridge University Press, 1959).

4. Böhme's contemporary, the English physician Robert Fludd, bemoaned his lack of inner knowledge and sought connection with the Rosicrucians because of their claim to possess it. The Rosicrucian clamor was a result of their claim to possess inner knowledge.

5. The Pietist movement of the eighteenth century evolved out of these study groups. Their existence and goals also help account for the favorable reception the Rosicrucian tracts generated in the early seventeenth century.

6. I use *Paracelsian* as a generic term to include a synthesis of sixteenth century Gnostic, Neoplatonic, alchemical, occult, and magical thought. By 1575, the intermingling of all these radical Renaissance philosophies is obvious. See Walter Pagel, *Paracelsus* (New York: S. Karger, 1958) and the numerous articles by him in *Ambix* 8 (1960), 9 (1961), 10 (1962), 16 (1969), and 21 (1974). Note also Allen Debus, *The Chemical Philosophy: Paracelsian Science and Medicine in the 16th and 17th Centuries*, 2 vols. (New York: Science History Publications, 1977) and *The English Paracelsians* (New York: F. Watts, 1965); A. E. Waite, Ed., *The Hermetic and Alchemical Writings of Aureolus Phillipus Bombast ab Hohenheim* (New York: University Books, 1967); R. Hookass, "Die Elementen Lehre des Paracelsus," *Janus* 39 (1936): 175-88 and *Janus* 41 (1937): 1-28; Francis Yates, *Giordano Bruno and the Hermetic Tradition* (New

York: Random House, 1969) and *The Rosicrucian Enlightenment* (Boulder, CO: Shambala, 1978); Lynn Thorndike, *The History of Magic and Experimental Science* (New York: Columbia University Press, 1941) 5:618-25.

7. Debus (1977, 63, 128) notes reprints of Paracelsus' works in 1603, 1605, 1616, and 1618. See also Thorndike (1941), 5:618-25.

8. See Peuckert (1961, 50 ff.) and J. J. Stoudt, *Sunrise to Eternity* (Philadelphia: University Press, 1957), 94-6.

9. Valentine Weigel's influence on Böhme is discussed in the next chapter. For Weigel see *Valentine Weigel Sämtliche Schriften.*, Ed. Will-Erich Peuckert, 7 Vols. (Stuttgart: Fr. Frommann's Verlag, 1957).

10. Pagel 1958, 226.

11. Paracelsus, "Athenians," 2: par. 13, in *Paracelsus Essential Readings*. Ed. and Trans. Nicholas Goodrick-Clark (New York: Crucible, 1990).

12. Ibid., par. 14.

13. Paracelsus, "Archidoxes," book 5, p. 37, in *Paracelsus Essential Readings*. Ed. and Trans. Nicholas Goodrick-Clark (New York: Crucible, 1990).

14. Böhme, *Mysterium Magnum*, Preface, par. 4.

15. Böhme, *Beschreibung der Drey Principien Göttliches Wesens*, chap. 5, par. 18.

16. Böhme, *Von der Geburt und Bezeichnung aller Wesens*, chap. 9, par. 1-4.

17. Böhme, *Principien*, chap. 7, par. 35. Also, the "outward nature of this visible comprehensible world is a manifestation or external birth of the inward spirit. Böhme, *Signatura*, chap. 3, par. 7.

18. Böhme, *Clavis*, par. 104.

19. Ibid., par. 115.

20. Pagel 1958, 224.

21. Böhme, *De Natura Rerum*, 178.

22. Ibid., 179.

23. Ralph Waldo Emerson, "The Over-Soul," in *Emerson's Essays* (New York: Thomas Y. Crowell, 1926), 203.

24. Jung called this involvement a psychological one. Meditation created a dialogue with the other in ourselves. Here "things pass from an unconscious potential state to a manifest one," Carl Jung, "The Psysic Nature of the Alchemical Work," in *Collected Works* (Princeton, NJ: Princeton University Press, 1968), 13:262.

25. Ibid., 13:288

26. Ibid., 13:234.

27. Ibid., 13:288.

28. Georg Wilhelm Friedrich Hegel, *The Phenomenology of Spirit*, Trans. A. V. Miller, analysis and Foreword J. N. Findlay (New York: Oxford University Press, 1976), 19-20.

29. Paracelsus 1990, "Das Buch Paragranum," 74 in *Paracelsus Essential Readings*. Ed. and Trans. Nicholas Goodrick-Clark (New York: Crucible, 1990).

30. Heyneman 1991, 7.

31. The Gadamer/Habermas debates were about whether reason could transcend sociolinguistic conditioning or if it was conditioned by it. Damasio (1994) tries to reassert the importance of feeling and emotion to the entire neurological process. But here, too, the ghosts of Socrates (reason = truth = happiness, as Nietzsche quipped) and Descartes influence patterns of thought. Damasio ties reason, emotion, and feeling together into an intimate web of relationships, but he still describes reason as the "higher realm" and feeling as the "lower realm," the "shadow of our evolutionary past." Might evolution occasionally be a contradiction in terms?

32. Gadamer 1977, 463.

33. Böhme, *Briefe*, 11, par. 8.

34. Böhme, *Mysterium Magnum*, chap. 10, par. 6.

35. Böhme, *Aurora*, chap. 25, par. 4. Also note *Principien*, "Vorrede," par. 15, and *Dreifach Leben*, chap. 1, par. 2ff.

36. Böhme, *Dreifach Leben*, chap. 1, par. 2.

37. Böhme, *Aurora*, chap. 25, par. 48.

38. Böhme, *Signatura*, chap. 3, par. 9.

CHAPTER 5

1. The best historical study of Schwenckfeld is R. Emmet McLaughlin, *Caspar Schwenckfeld, Reluctant Radical* (New Haven, CT: Yale University Press, 1986). See also Selina G. Schultz, *Caspar Schwenckfeld von Ossig* (Philadelphia: Schwenckfelder Church, 1947); Karl Eck, *Schwenckfeld, Luther, und der Gedanke einer apostolishen Reformation* (Berlin: Verlag Martin Warneck, 1911); Rufus M. Jones, *Spiritual Reformers in the 16th and 17th Centuries* (London: Macmillan, 1928). Unless otherwise stated, quotations and translations from Schwenckfeld are by Schultz and refer to *Corpus Schwenckfeldianorum*, Ed. E.E.S. Johnson (Leipzig: Breitkopf and Hartel, 1919).

2. Schwenckfeld, *Corpus*, 2:132.

3. Ibid., 2:132-3.

4. Ibid., 2:135.

5. McLaughlin 1986, 73.

Notes

6. Schwenckfeld, *Corpus*, 2:138.
7. Ibid., 2:255. The entire text, quoted on 240-257, is a letter entitled "Vom richten Verstande der Wort: Das ist mein Leib/Das ist mein Blut."
8. Ibid., 2:257.
9. Ibid.
10. Ibid., 2:258.
11. Jones, *Spiritual Reformers*, 7-9.
12. Schwenckfeld, *Corpus*, 4:524.
13. Ibid., 2:528.
14. Ibid., 4:775-76. Also see McLaughlin 1986, 44-5.
15. Ibid., 2: 592:26-593:3. Quoted by McLaughlin 1986, 97.
16. The Heideggerian word "releasement" seems appropriate here. Although I have not researched the connection between Heidegger and spiritualist thought, the epistemological relationships are striking. John Caputo defines releasement as a "thinking which proceeds in freedom from the constructs of the thinking subject, unobstructed by sugjective constructions, a thinking which has deconstructed the works of subjectivity—precisely in order to gain access to the sphere which they obstruct." John D. Caputo, *Radical Hermeneutics* (Bloomington: Indiana University Press, 1987), 99. For Heidegger and mysticism, see Caputo, *The Mystical Element in Heidegger* (Athens: Ohio University Press, 1978).
17. McLaughlin 1986, 48.
18. Ibid., 45. This issue is devloped more fully by Böhme and will be discussed in the latter part of this chapter.
19. Sebastian Franck, *Chronica und Beschreibung der Turkey* (Nürnberg: 1530) K, 3 b. Quoted in Jones 1928, 49.
20. See Jones 1928, 50.
21. Valentine Weigel, "Ein Buchlein vom Wahren Seligmachenden Glauben," in *Sämtliche Schriften* (1957)3:12-4 (hereafter cited as "Buchlein").
22. Weigel, "Vom Ort der Welt." *Sämtliche Schriften* (1957) 1:46.
23. Ibid., 1:51.
24. Ibid., 1:52. Also see *Buchlein*, 5:18.
25. Valentine Weigel, "Kürzer Bericht & Anleitung zur Deutschen Theologie," *Sämtliche Schriften* 3:95, (hereafter cited as *Kürzer Bericht*).
26. Ibid., 94.
27. Weigel *Buchlein*, 3:19.
28. Steven Ozment, *Mysticism and Dissent* (New Haven: Yale University Press, 1973), 215.

29. Valentine Weigel, *Astrology Theologized* (London: George Redway, 1886), 52. Possibly apocryphal.

30. Weigel, *Kürzer Bericht*, 94.

31. See Karl Jöel, *Der Ursprung der Naturphilosophies aus dem Geiste der Mystic* (Basal: F. Reinhart, 1903).

32. See Robert Fludd, "Summo Buon" in *A Rosicrucian Anthology*, Ed. Paul M. Allen (New York: Rudolf Steiner, 1968), 351; Andre Libavias, *Wohlmeinendes Bedencken von der FAMA und Confession der Brüderschaft dass Rose Creuz* (Erfurt: Johann Rohbock, 1616), 18-24; Johann Andreä "Christianopolis" and "Chemical Wedding" in *A Rosicruciun Anthology*, trans. Felix Held (Oxford: Oxford University Press, 1916), 138.

33. See Stoudt 1957, 50.

34. Will-Erick Peuckert, "Das Leben Jacob Böhme." In *Jacob Böhme Sämtliche Schrifter* (Stuttgart: Fr. Frommann's Verlag 1961), 10:29.

35. Ibid., 10:31.

36. Will-Erick Peuckert, *Das Rosenkreutz* (Berlin: Erich Schmidt Verlag, 1973), 228-31.

37. Böhme, *Briefe*, letter 12, par. 52-64.

38. Ibid., par. 52.

39. Ibid., par. 54-58.

40. Ibid., par. 52.

41. Ibid., chap. 10, par. 28-30.

42. See David Walsh, *The Mysticism of Innerworldly Fulfillment* (Gainesville: University Presses of Florida, 1983).

43. Böhme, *Mysterium Magnum*, chap. 5, par. 14.

44. Böhme, *Aurora*, chap. 22, par. 15.

45. Ibid., chap. 22, par. 9.

46. Ibid., chap. 25, par. 1-2.

47. Ibid.

48. Ibid., chap. 22, par. 15.

49. Galileo 1967, 144-7.

CHAPTER 6

1. Böhme, *Aurora*, chap. 25, par. 65. Note also *Von dreifach Leben des Menschen* chap. 9, par. 9.

2. Ibid., par. 66.

3. Ibid., par. 67.

4. Giordano Bruno died at the stake in 1600, proclaiming the wonderfulness of an infinite universe.

5. Böhme, *Aurora*, chap. 19, par. 3-4.
6. Ibid., chap. 25, par. 1-2.
7. Ibid., par. 1-3.
8. Ibid., par. 19.
9. Ibid., par. 6-10.
10. Langdon Gilkey, *Naming the Whirlwind*. (New York: Bobbs Merrill, 1977).
11. Recent examples: Davies 1992 and Tipler 1995.
12. Böhme, *Aurora*, chap. 25, par 1-2.
13. Ibid., chap. 22, par. 15
14. Ibid., chap. 23, par. 86.

CHAPTER 7

1. This position was recently assumed by Stephen Hawking, *A Brief History of Time* (New York: Bantam, 1990).
2. Böhme, *Mysterium Magnum*, vol. 3, chap. 1, par. 2. The twentieth century philosopher Alfred North Whitehead (*Process and Reality*, New York: Free Press, 1978) has described this aspect of God in a similar way: He says God must be the "primordial created fact ... the unconditioned conceptual valuation of the entire multiplicity of eternal objects," 32.
3. Böhme, *Clavis*, par. 2.
4. Böhme, *Mysterium Magnum*, chap. 4, par. 1.
5. Lewis White-Beck, *Early German Philosophy: Kant and his Predecessors* (Cambridge, MA: Harvard University Press, 1969) pointed out that Böhme was similar to Eckhart "in attributing an inner tension or struggle or anguish to God," 155. I do not feel this is quite accurate. God, before the process of creation begins, is peaceful. Only after It desires to create Itself does a tension develop. That tension is a result of the processes of creation. The desire to be more than It is starts the tension. Creation is advanced through tension, but tension is not inherent in God.
6. Böhme, *Mysterium Magnum*, chap. 3, par. 5.
7. Ibid., chap. 3, par. 6-7.
8. Ibid., par. 8.
9. Böhme, *Von Sechs Theosophischen Puncten*. chap. 1, par. 9. Hereafter, "Puncten."
10. Ibid., chap. 1, par. 31. Frederick Copelston noted this idea in *A History of Philosophy* (Garden City, NY: 1960), 6:81.
11. Böhme, *Menschwerdung*, chap. 2, par. 3.
12. Böhme, *Mysterium Magnum*, chap. 3, par. 4.

13. Böhme used various other synonyms to describe the same idea. Herman Vetterling, *The Illuminate of Görlitz*, (Hildesheim: Gerstenberg Verlag, 1978) lists the following: The Seven Powers, the Generations, the Life Forms, the Fountain Spirits, the Essences, the Species, the Births, the spirits of life, the Astral Spirits, the Roots, the Wheels, and the Seven Mothers. Böhme's properties should not be confused with Platonic forms, which, while invisible and eternal, did not have generative power.

14. Böhme, *Mysterium Magnum*, chap. 3, par. 21.

15. The biologist Theodosius Dobzhansky's (*The Biology of Ultimate Concern*, New York: New American Library, 1967) discussion of evolution in terms of novelty sounds similar to Böhme's overriding conception. Dobzhansky stresses the epigenetic character of evolution.

16. Böhme, *Clavis*, par. 28.

17. Böhme, *Mysterium Magnum*, chap. 6, par. 22.

18. This field concept seems similar to that discussed most recently by the German theologian Wolfhart Pannenberg, *Toward a Theology of Nature* (Louisville, KY: Westminister/John Knox Press, 1993). Paul Tillich,*Systematic Theology* (Chicago: University of Chicago Press, 1951-53) and Polanyi 1964 develop similar ideas of a field concept. For Polanyi, the field concept provides a description of all aspects of organic life, including its connection to nature. We can count Teilhard de Chardin, *The Phenomenon of Man*, (New York: Harper, 1959) here as well.

19. Böhme, *Mysterium Magnum*, chap. 3, par. 9.

20. Ibid., chap. 3, par. 10.

21. Ibid.

22. Ibid., chap. 3, par. 11.

23. Ibid., chap. 3, par. 12.

24. Ibid. Also see chap. 6, par. 16.

25. Ibid., chap 3, par. 15.

26. Böhme, *Clavis*, par. 48.

27. Ibid., par. 58.

28. Ibid., par. 69. Also see Böhme, *Mysterium*, chap. 5, par. 14.

29. Böhme, *Mysterium*, chap. 5, par. 11 and chap. 6, par. 19.

30. Ibid., chap. 5, par. 19.

31. Ibid., chap. 6, par. 3.

32. The image of a snake biting its tail often signifies the whole or sphere that surrounds the earth. Joseph Campbell, *The Masks of God: Occidental Mythology*, (New York: Penguin, 1964), states that "When imagined as biting it tail ... it suggests the waters that in all archaic

cosmologies surround—as well as lie beneath and permeate—the floating circular island Earth," 10.
33. Böhme, *Mysterium*, chap. 6, par. 3.
34. Ibid., par. 21.
35. According to Joseph Campbell, then, Böhme's view would be archaic, Lunar, and feminine as opposed to patriarchal: "The patriarchal point of view is distinguished from the earlier archaic view by its setting apart of all pairs-of-opposites ... as though they were absolutes in themselves and not merely aspects of the larger entity of life. Campbell 1964, 26-27.
36. Böhme, *Mysterium*, chap. 6, par. 9.
37. Ibid., chap. 10, par 5.
38. Ibid., chap. 8, par. 12.
39. Ibid., chap. 7, par. 18.
40. Ibid., chap. 11, par. 33.
41. Ibid., chap. 14, par. 10-11.
42. Ibid., chap. 11, par. 2.
43. Ibid., chap. 12-16.
44. Ibid., chap. 12, par. 3.
45. Böhme, *Clavis*, par. 104.
46. Böhme, *Mysterium*, chap. 12, par. 34.
47. Ibid., chap. 2, par. 7.

CHAPTER 8

1. In the *Symposium* Plato has Eryximacus describe the world in somewhat similar, but much less complex terms, 186a-188d.
2. Recent studies (see Verlyn Klinkenborg, *New York Times Magazine*, January 5, 1997, 26 ff.) that recreated the sleep patterns of primitive peoples show that during the twelve to fourteen hours of winter darkness prehistoric peoples slept, a specific pattern of sleep occurred: Five hours of REM sleep associated with dreaming was followed by a period of quiet wakefulness. As humans have become more pragmatic and busy, sleep has become a nuisance. Dominating night and season with artificial light and shelter, our sleeping patterns, compressed and consolidated, do not allow us the dreaming states of our early forefathers. Sleep investigators have suggested that this might help explain the observation that modern humans seem to have lost touch with the wellspring of myths and fantasies. Again, the whole sense of understanding derived from subrational areas of the brain has been pushed aside in the modern world. There might be a relationship between this state of sleep and meditative and mystical understanding.

3. Böhme, *Dreifach Leben*, chap. 8, par. 1.
4. Böhme, *Mysterium Magnum*, chap. 5, par. 3-4.
5. Böhme, *Aurora*, chap. 21, par. 77-78.
6. Ibid., chap. 25, par. 25.
7. Böhme, *Clavis*, par. 105.
8. Böhme, *Mysterium Magnum*, chap. 2, par. 7.
9. Böhme, *Puncten*, chap. 11, par. 28.
10. Böhme, *Aurora*, chap. 8, par. 65.
11. Böhme, *Puncten*, chap. 3, par. 55. Also see *Clavis*, par. 110.
12. Böhme, *Aurora*, chap. 21, par. 81.
13. Böhme, *Principien*, "Vorrede," par. 13.
14. Böhme, *Dreifach Leben*, chap. 7, par. 7.
15. Again, see Whitehead 1978, 342-51 and 31-4.
16. Similar ideas are found in Nicholas of Cusa and Hegel. Böhme's ideas on creation are similar to Cusa's insofar as both show the universe as the unfolding of God and the individual parts of reality as mirroring the whole. See Copelston 1963, 3:2, 29-53. A modern philosopher with similar ideas on the oppositional character of reality is Whitehead. "In our cosmological construction we are, therefore, left with the final opposites, joy and sorrow, good and evil, disjunction and conjunction—that is to say the many in the one—flux and permanence, greatness and triviality, freedom and necessity, God and the World. In this list, the pairs of opposites are in experience with a certain ultimate directness of intuition, except in the case of the last pair. God and the World introduce the note of interpretation," Whitehead 1978, 341.

INDEX

Alchemy and occult philosophy, 52-60
Alighieri, Dante, 29
Andreä, Johann, 70-71
Arndt, Johann, 71
Aristotle, 50, 107
Baader, Franz Xavier von, 13
Bacon, Francis, 12-13, 50, 59, 61
    epistemology and methodology, 20-21
    sense experience, 23
Blake, William, 9, 13, 15, 50
Böhme, Jacob,
    alchemy and, 55-60
    as a modern man, 82-85
    background, 2, 11-14, 60-62
    the Church and, 71-73
    Copernicus and, 13-15, 74-75, 80-82
    Eternal Nature and, 15, 50, 91-100, 103-104
    External Nature and, 94-97, 100-101, 104-106
    Galileo and, 61, 74-76, 83
    God, 79-85, 100-102, 107-108
    historical importance, 12-14, 42
    historical knowledge and, 13, 42, 50-51
    mystical experiences, 31-34, 37, 40-43, 48, 88-91
    mystical knowledge, 41, 50, 79, 81-85, 88
    Nietzsche, Friedrich, and, 77-78, 83
    Paracelsus and, 52-60, 71, 79
    revelation of, 93
    Schwenckfeld, Caspar, and, 63, 68, 72-79
    Scientific Revolution and, 12, 74-76, 83-85
    spiritualism and, 48, 63-73, 79
    theory of evolution, 104, 110
    Weigel, Valentine, and, 71
Browning, Robert, 13
Cave painting, 38-39
Conceptual orientation, 32
    confusion and, 17
    experience and, 15-24, 38-41
    in the humanities, 28
    limits of, 28, 32
    science and, 17, 28
Copernicus, 13, 31, 74, 80-82
Damasio, Antonio R., 40-42
Deikman, Arthur, 41
Descartes, René, 15, 61
    epistemology and methodology, 21, 24
    sense experience and, 29
Duerr, Hans Peter, and rites of passage, 33

Eckhart, Meister, 11, 15, 66, 69
Einstein, Albert, 93
Emerson, Ralph Waldo, 55
Ender, Michael, 71
Fludd, Robert, 71
Formula of Concord, 12, 51, 72
Franck, Sebastian, 68
Freud, Sigmund, and religion, 6-7
Galileo, 12, 14-15, 58, 60, 75-76, 83
    Böhme and, 75-76
    the Church and, 7
    epistemology methodology, 21-26
Ginzburg, Carlo, 51
Gnosticism, 52, 59
God,
    evolution of, 92-98
    nature and, 99-101, 103, 105-106
Görlitz, 11-13, 52-53, 71, 78
Harvey, William, 12, 14, 61
Hawking, Stephen, 85, 93
Hegel, G.W.F., 12-13, 15, 41, 50, 60
Heidegger, Martin, 15
Heisenberg, Werner, 25
Heraclitus, change, and truth, 32
Heyneman, Martha, 36-37
Humanities,
    experience and, 27-32
    knowledge and, 27
    values and, 28
Hume, David, 91
Jung, Carl Gustav, 59
Kepler, Johannes, 12, 74
Law, William, 13
Lawrence, D. H., 15, 50
    experience and, 32
Leibniz, Gottfried Wilhelm, 36, 63
Libavius, Andrea, 71
Luther, Martin, 80
    differences between Caspar Schwenckfeld and, 63-66
Möller, Martin, 12, 53, 71
Musil, Robert, and the "other condition," 9, 33
Mystical experience
    as existential knowledge, 11, 35, 39-43

Böhme, Jacob, and, 31-34, 37, 40-48, 88-91
    the brain and, 40-42
    description of, 1-2, 31, 33-45, 88
    issue of, 35
    means to, 33, 38-41, 78
    meditation and, 39
    origins of, 10-11
    versus rational experience, 35, 40-42
Neo-Platonism, 53-54, 64, 92-93, 104
Newton, Issac, 63, 83
    scientific knowledge and, 23
Nietzsche, Friedrich, 48, 77-78, 80, 82-83
Novak, Philip, and mystical experience, 34
Pagel, Walter, 53
Paracelsus, 12, 15, 48-50, 52-54, 107
Pascal, Blaise, 36
Pomeranus of Wittenberg, 63-65
Pragmatic reasoning,
    aim of, 3-4
    compared to mystical activity, 41
    concept formation and, 38-41
    in science, 5
    power of, 4
    problems with, 9
Rational consciousness,
    in evolution, 3-6
    limits of, 5-6
    Neanderthals, rocket scientists, and, 3
Reason in the medieval period, 20
Religion,
    Freud, Sigmund, critique of, 6-7
    rational consciousness and, 7-8
    science and, 20-21
    versus the religious, 7
Religious,
    difference between religion and, 7-8
    experience, 7-9, 44
Richter, Gregor, 73
Roethke, Theodore, 13
Rosicrucians, 70-71

Royal Society, the, and nomenclature, 22-23
Russell, Bertrand, 31
Schwenckfeld, Caspar, 12, 48, 51, 68
  epistemology, 63-69
  differences with Martin Luther, 63-66
Science,
  as rational consciousness, 4-6, 25
  concept formulation and, 20-21
  epistemology and methodology, 5, 19-27
  experience and, 19-25
  historical knowledge, 25-26
  intellectual framework, 5, 19-26
  mathematics and, 22-24
  values and, 25-27
  versus religion, 5-7
Scientific Revolution, x, 20-26
Steiner, George,
  symbols, signs, and knowledge, 30-31
  spirit and art, 32
Weigel, Valentine, 53, 68-70
  knowledge of nature and, 70
Wittgenstein, Ludwig, 15
  chaos and truth, 32
Wulff, Lee, relating to nature, 38
Zwingli, Ulrich, 64